# My Little Salmon Cookbook

## Only the Best Salmon Recipes Every Chef Should Know!

By
BookSumo Press

Published by
http://www.booksumo.com

# ENJOY THE RECIPES?

## KEEP ON COOKING
### WITH 6 MORE FREE COOKBOOKS!

Visit our website and simply enter your email address to join the club and receive your 6 cookbooks.

http://booksumo.com/magnet

https://www.instagram.com/booksumopress/

https://www.facebook.com/booksumo/

# LEGAL NOTES

# Table of Contents

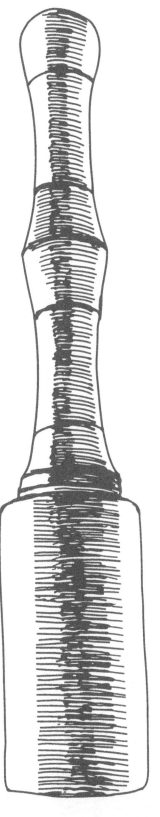

# Maggie's
# Favorite Chowder

🥣 Prep Time: 15 mins
🕐 Total Time: 45 mins

Servings per Recipe: 8
| | |
|---|---|
| Calories | 490 kcal |
| Carbohydrates | 26.5 g |
| Cholesterol | 104 mg |
| Fat | 25.9 g |
| Protein | 38.6 g |
| Sodium | 1140 mg |

## Ingredients

3 tbsps butter
3/4 cup diced onion
1/2 cup diced celery
1 tsp garlic powder
2 cups diced potatoes
2 carrots, diced
2 cups chicken broth
1 tsp salt
1 tsp ground black pepper

1 tsp dried dill weed
2 cans salmon
1 can evaporated milk
1 can creamed corn
1/2 pound Cheddar cheese, shredded

## Directions

1. Cook onion, garlic powder and celery in hot butter until you see that the onions are tender before adding potatoes, salt, carrots, broth, pepper and dill, and bringing all this to boil.

2. Cook it covered for about 20 minutes before stirring in salmon, cheese, evaporated milk and corn.

3. Heat it up for a few minutes (2 to 4 mins) before serving.

# GRILLED
# Salmon

Prep Time: 15 mins
Total Time: 2 hrs 31 min

Servings per Recipe: 6
| | |
|---|---|
| Calories | 318 kcal |
| Carbohydrates | 13.2 g |
| Cholesterol | 56 mg |
| Fat | 20.1 g |
| Protein | 20.5 g |
| Sodium | 1092 mg |

## Ingredients

1 1/2 pounds salmon fillets
lemon pepper to taste
garlic powder to taste
salt to taste
1/3 cup soy sauce
1/3 cup brown sugar

1/3 cup water
1/4 cup vegetable oil

## Directions

1. At first you need to set a grill at medium heat and put some oil before starting anything else.
2. Coat a mixture of salmon fillets, salt, lemon pepper and garlic powder with a mixture of soy sauce, vegetable oil and water in a plastic bag before refrigerating it for at least 2 hours.
3. Now cook salmon on the preheated grill for about 8 minutes each side.
4. Serve.

# Buttered
# Salmon

Prep Time: 5 mins
Total Time: 30 mins

Servings per Recipe: 4
| | |
|---|---|
| Calories | 262 kcal |
| Carbohydrates | 0.7 g |
| Cholesterol | 82 mg |
| Fat | 18.1 g |
| Protein | 22.8 g |
| Sodium | 254 mg |

## Ingredients

1 pound salmon fillets or steaks
1/4 tsp salt
1/2 tsp ground black pepper
1 tsp onion powder

1 tsp dried dill weed
2 tbsps butter

## Directions

1. Set your oven at 400 degrees before doing anything else.
2. Coat salmon with salt, onion powder, pepper, butter and dill very thoroughly before placing it in the oven.
3. Bake this in the preheated oven for about 25 minutes.
4. Serve.

# PARMESAN
# and Tomato Salmon

 Prep Time: 15 mins

Total Time: 45 mins

Servings per Recipe: 4

| | |
|---|---|
| Calories | 955 kcal |
| Carbohydrates | 85 g |
| Cholesterol | 122 mg |
| Fat | 48.7 g |
| Protein | 41.9 g |
| Sodium | 631 mg |

## Ingredients

1 cup uncooked long grain white rice
2 cups water
2 1/2 tbsps garlic oil
2 fillets salmon
salt and pepper to taste
1/2 tsp dried dill weed
1/4 tsp paprika to taste
2 fresh tomatoes, diced
1 1/2 tsps minced garlic

1 tsp lemon juice
3 tbsps diced fresh parsley
1/4 cup grated Parmesan cheese
2 tbsps butter
4 dashes hot pepper sauce
Check All Add to Shopping List

## Directions

1. Bring a mixture of rice and water to boil before cooking this at low heat for about 20 minutes.
2. Cook salmon seasoned with paprika, salt, dill and pepper in hot garlic oil for about 2 minutes before adding tomatoes, lemon juice and garlic, and cooking all this until the salmon is tender.
3. Stir in parsley, butter, Parmesan cheese, and hot pepper before cooking all this for another two minutes.
4. Pour it over cooked rice for serving.

# *Ginger*
# Sesame Salmon

🥣 Prep Time: 10 mins

🕐 Total Time: 2 hrs 18 mins

Servings per Recipe: 4

| | |
|---|---|
| Calories | 664 kcal |
| Carbohydrates | 11.2 g |
| Cholesterol | 112 mg |
| Fat | 50.4 g |
| Protein | 40.9 g |
| Sodium | 1599 mg |

## Ingredients

1/4 cup balsamic vinegar
1/4 cup lemon juice
1/4 cup soy sauce
1 tsp salt
1 tbsp brown sugar
1 1/2 tsps ground ginger
1 tsp paprika
1 tsp black pepper
1 tsp crushed red pepper flakes

4 cloves garlic, minced
1/4 cup diced green onions
1 tsp sesame oil
1/2 cup peanut oil
8 skinless, boneless salmon fillets

## Directions

1. At first you need to set a grill at medium heat and put some oil before starting anything else.
2. Coat salmon with a mixture of balsamic vinegar, red pepper flakes, lemon juice, pepper, soy sauce with salt, ground ginger, paprika, garlic, green onions, brown sugar, sesame oil and peanut oil in a plastic bag very thoroughly before refrigerating it for at least 2 hours.
3. Now cook salmon on the preheated grill for about 4 minutes each side.
4. Serve.

# LEMON DILL
# Salmon

Prep Time: 15 mins
Total Time: 40 mins

Servings per Recipe: 6
Calories                169 kcal
Carbohydrates           2.1 g
Cholesterol             50 mg
Fat                     6.7 g
Protein                 24.5 g
Sodium                  48 mg

## Ingredients

1 1/2 pounds salmon fillet
salt and pepper to taste
3 cloves garlic, minced
1 sprig fresh dill, chopped
5 slices lemon

5 sprigs fresh dill weed
2 green onions, chopped

## Directions

1.  Set your oven at 450 degrees and lightly oil the baking dish before doing anything else.
2.  Coat salmon with a mixture of salt, dill, pepper, scallions and garlic very thoroughly before placing some lemon slices and a sprig of dill on top of the salmon.
3.  Cover it up with aluminum foil before placing it in the oven.
4.  Bake this in the preheated oven for about 25 minutes.
5.  Serve.

# Ginger and Grapefruit Salmon

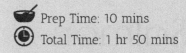

Prep Time: 10 mins
Total Time: 1 hr 50 mins

Servings per Recipe: 1
Calories            221 kcal
Carbohydrates       2.9 g
Cholesterol         66 mg
Fat                 12.2 g
Protein             23.4 g
Sodium              1040 mg

## Ingredients

1/2 grapefruit, juiced
3 1/3 ounces soy sauce
1/4 tsp salt
1/2 tsp garlic powder

1/4 tsp ground ginger
1 whole salmon fillet

## Directions

1. Set your oven at 400 degrees before doing anything else.
2. Coat salmon with a mixture of grapefruit juice, ground ginger, soy sauce, garlic powder and salt before covering it with plastic wrap and refrigerating it for at least one hour.
3. Bake this in the preheated oven for about 40 minutes.
4. Serve.

# RASPBERRY
# Salmon

 Prep Time: 10 mins
Total Time: 45 mins

Servings per Recipe: 4
| | |
|---|---|
| Calories | 193 kcal |
| Carbohydrates | 19.4 g |
| Cholesterol | 41 mg |
| Fat | 5.4 g |
| Protein | 15.9 g |
| Sodium | 209 mg |

## Ingredients

2 (6 ounce) salmon filets, skin on
1/4 cup barbeque sauce
1/4 cup seedless raspberry jam

## Directions

1.  Set your oven at 400 degrees before doing anything else.
2.  Coat salmon with a mixture of barbeque sauce and raspberry jam very thoroughly.
3.  Bake this in the preheated oven for about 25 minutes, while brushing it with the same mixture after 15 minutes of baking time.
4.  Serve.

# *Honey* Mustard Salmon

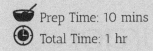

Prep Time: 10 mins
Total Time: 1 hr

Servings per Recipe: 6
| | |
|---|---|
| Calories | 303 kcal |
| Carbohydrates | 9.2 g |
| Cholesterol | 75 mg |
| Fat | 19.2 g |
| Protein | 23.3 g |
| Sodium | 192 mg |

## Ingredients

1 tbsp butter, melted
1 tbsp vegetable oil
1 tbsp Worcestershire sauce
2 tbsps honey mustard

1 tbsp brown sugar
1 tbsp garlic powder
1 pound salmon fillet

## Directions

1. The distance of your rack should be about 5 inch from the heat source before preheating you broiler.
2. Coat salmon with a mixture of melted butter, brown sugar, vegetable oil, Worcestershire sauce, honey mustard sauce, and garlic powder in a bowl very thoroughly before covering it up and refrigerating it for at least 45 minutes.
3. Now cook this salmon under the preheated broiler for about 12 minutes before letting it cool down for 5 minutes.
4. Serve.

# SALMON
# Burger

Prep Time: 10 mins
Total Time: 25 mins

Servings per Recipe: 4
Calories               268 kcal
Carbohydrates          12.9 g
Cholesterol            92 mg
Fat                    10.9 g
Protein                27.8 g
Sodium                 484 mg

## Ingredients

1 can salmon, liquid removed and
flaked
3/4 cup rolled oats
1/2 onion, sliced
1 egg

1/2 lemon, juiced
1 tbsp Dijon mustard
salt and ground black pepper to taste
1 tsp vegetable oil

## Directions

1. Make four patties from a mixture of salmon, mustard, oats, onion, egg, lemon juice, salt, and black pepper very neatly.
2. Fry these patties in hot oil for about seven minutes each side.
3. Serve.

# Brown Sugar
# Salmon

🍲 Prep Time: 15 mins
🕐 Total Time: 1 hr 23 mins

Servings per Recipe: 5

| | |
|---|---|
| Calories | 323 kcal |
| Carbohydrates | 11.7 g |
| Cholesterol | 101 mg |
| Fat | 18.9 g |
| Protein | 24.5 g |
| Sodium | 308 mg |

## Ingredients

1/4 cup butter, melted
1/4 cup brown sugar
1 tbsp soy sauce
2 tbsps lemon juice

2 tbsps white wine
1 1/4 pounds salmon fillets

## Directions

1. At first you need to set a grill to medium heat and put some oil before starting anything else.
2. Coat salmon with a mixture of melted butter, lemon juice, brown sugar, soy sauce and white wine in a plastic bag before refrigerating it for at least one hour.
3. Now cook salmon on the preheated grill for about 4 minutes each side, while brushing salmon with the marinade in all this time.
4. Serve.

# SALMON
# Salad

 Prep Time: 15 mins

Total Time: 15 mins

Servings per Recipe: 4

| | |
|---|---|
| Calories | 248 kcal |
| Carbohydrates | 2.2 g |
| Cholesterol | 43 mg |
| Fat | 17.2 g |
| Protein | 20.4 g |
| Sodium | 571 mg |

## Ingredients

2 cans pink salmon, liquid removed
1/2 cup finely sliced green onions
1/2 cup finely diced celery
1/4 cup mayonnaise
3/4 tsp lemon juice

3/4 tsp dried dill
3/4 tsp seasoned salt

## Directions

1. Combine all the ingredients very thoroughly before refrigerating it.
2. Serve.

# *Mushroom* Salmon

🥣 Prep Time: 15 mins
🕐 Total Time: 45 mins

Servings per Recipe: 6
| | |
|---|---|
| Calories | 217 kcal |
| Carbohydrates | 2.5 g |
| Cholesterol | 66 mg |
| Fat | 12.2 g |
| Protein | 22.7 g |
| Sodium | 597 mg |

## Ingredients

6 (4 ounce) fillets salmon
1 (.7 ounce) package dry Italian-style salad dressing mix
1/2 cup water

2 tbsps lemon juice
1 cup fresh sliced mushrooms

## Directions

1. Set your oven at 400 degrees before doing anything else.
2. Coat salmon with a mixture of water, dressing mix and lemon juice before placing sliced mushrooms on top.
3. Bake this in the preheated oven covered for about 15 minutes and uncovered for additional 15 minutes.
4. Serve.

# HEALTHY
# Salmon

Prep Time: 10 mins
Total Time: 25 mins

Servings per Recipe: 1

| | |
|---|---|
| Calories | 219 kcal |
| Carbohydrates | 2.6 g |
| Cholesterol | 67 mg |
| Fat | 12.3 g |
| Protein | 22.9 g |
| Sodium | 68 mg |

## Ingredients

1 pound salmon fillet
1 onion, sliced into rings
freshly ground black pepper

## Directions

1. At first you need to set a grill to medium heat and put some oil before starting anything else.
2. Wrap salmon up around the aluminum foil after adding some pepper.
3. Now cook wrapped salmon on the preheated grill for about 15 minutes each side.
4. Serve.

# *Salmon* Croquettes

🥣 Prep Time: 10 mins
🕐 Total Time: 20 mins

Servings per Recipe: 4
| | |
|---|---|
| Calories | 435 kcal |
| Carbohydrates | 12.2 g |
| Cholesterol | 130 mg |
| Fat | 30.9 g |
| Protein | 27.9 g |
| Sodium | 360 mg |

## Ingredients

1 (6 ounce) can salmon, liquid removed and flaked
1 egg
1/4 cup finely diced celery
1/4 cup sliced green onion
1 tbsp diced fresh dill weed

1/2 tsp garlic powder
1/3 cup wheat germ
3 tbsps olive oil

## Directions

1. Form small balls from a mixture of salmon, green onion, egg, celery, and dill and finally garlic powder before coating with wheat germ.
2. Now fry these balls in hot oil for about 10 minutes, while turning when needed.
3. Serve.

# JAPANESE STYLE
# Salmon

 Prep Time: 10 mins

Total Time: 3 hrs 20 mins

Servings per Recipe: 4

| | |
|---|---|
| Calories | 333 kcal |
| Carbohydrates | 22.3 g |
| Cholesterol | 67 mg |
| Fat | 15.8 g |
| Protein | 24.1 g |
| Sodium | 764 mg |

## Ingredients

1 pound salmon fillets
1/3 cup brown sugar, divided
2 tsps lemon pepper, divided
1 tsp garlic powder, divided
1/3 cup low sodium soy sauce

1 tbsp olive oil
1 (1 inch) piece fresh ginger root, minced

## Directions

1. Heat up your broiler first, before starting anything else.
2. Coat salmon with brown sugar, garlic powder and lemon pepper very neatly, and set it aside.
3. Combine soy sauce, garlic powder, remaining brown sugar, ginger, olive oil and lemon pepper over medium heat in a saucepan before stirring in some orange juice.
4. Coat salmon with this marinade very thoroughly in a plastic bag before placing it in the refrigerator for at least three hours.
5. Now cook in the preheated broiler for 4 mins.
6. Turn the salmon around and cook it for another four minutes.
7. Let it cool down for five minutes before serving.

# The Easiest
# Salmon Cakes

🥣 Prep Time: 15 mins
🕐 Total Time: 25 mins

Servings per Recipe: 8

| | |
|---|---|
| Calories | 263 kcal |
| Carbohydrates | 10.8 g |
| Cholesterol | 95 mg |
| Fat | 12.3 g |
| Protein | 27.8 g |
| Sodium | 782 mg |

## Ingredients

2 (14.75 ounce) cans salmon, liquid removed and flaked
3/4 cup Italian-seasoned panko
1/2 cup minced fresh parsley
2 eggs, beaten
2 green onions, chopped
2 tsps seafood seasoning
1 1/2 tsps ground black pepper
1 1/2 tsps garlic powder

3 tbsps Worcestershire sauce
3 tbsps grated Parmesan cheese
2 tbsps Dijon mustard
2 tbsps creamy salad dressing
1 tbsp olive oil, or as needed, divided

## Directions

1. Make eight nicely shaped patties from a mixture of salmon, Worcestershire sauce, panko, parsley, garlic powder, eggs, black pepper, green onions, seafood seasoning, Parmesan cheese, Dijon mustard, and creamy salad dressing.

2. Cook these patties in batches in hot olive oil for about 7 minutes each side.

3. Serve.

# SALMON
# of Lemon and Pepper

Prep Time: 15 mins
Total Time: 23 mins

Servings per Recipe: 4
Calories                239 kcal
Carbohydrates           0.9 g
Cholesterol             71 mg
Fat                     16.7 g
Protein                 20.2 g
Sodium                  892 mg

## Ingredients

4 (4 ounce) salmon fillets
2 tbsps butter, melted
2 tbsps soy sauce

lemon pepper to taste

## Directions

1. Heat up the broiler and lightly oil the grate.
2. Coat salmon with a mixture of melted butter and soy sauce before adding some lemon pepper.
3. Now cook this salmon under the preheated broiler for about 8 minutes before letting it cool down for 5 minutes.
4. Serve.

# *Oriental*
# Salmon

Prep Time: 15 mins
Total Time: 1 hr 45 mins

Servings per Recipe: 8

| | |
|---|---|
| Calories | 388 kcal |
| Carbohydrates | 39.6 g |
| Cholesterol | 51 mg |
| Fat | 12 g |
| Protein | 27.9 g |
| Sodium | 279 mg |

## Ingredients

2 pounds salmon fillets, with skin
2 tbsps olive oil
2 tbsps rice vinegar
2 tbsps soy sauce
1 tbsp packed brown sugar
2 cloves garlic, minced
1 pinch ground black pepper
2 tbsps minced onion

1 tbsp sesame oil
2 cups long-grain white rice
1 tsp dried dill weed
3 cups water

## Directions

1. Set your oven at 350 degrees before doing anything else.
2. Coat salmon with a mixture of olive oil, brown sugar, rice vinegar, soy sauce, onion, garlic, pepper, and sesame oil very thoroughly before covering it up and refrigerating it for at least an hour.
3. Bring a mixture of dill weed, rice and water to boil before turning down the heat to low and cooking it for 20 minutes.
4. Place salmon in the oven and bake in the preheated oven for about 30 minutes.
5. Pour this over the cooked rice for serving.
6. Enjoy.

# HEALTHY
# Frittata

 Prep Time: 15 mins

Total Time: 35 mins

Servings per Recipe: 4
Calories                  241.7 kcal
Cholesterol               30.1mg
Sodium                    851.7mg
Carbohydrates             27.6g
Protein                   23.3g

## Ingredients

1 C. egg substitute
1/4 C. nonfat milk
1 tbsp fresh dill, chopped
3/4 tsp salt
1/4 tsp ground pepper
1/2 lb fresh white mushroom, sliced
1 (15 oz.) cans white potatoes, drained
and sliced

1 small red pepper, seeded and minced
1/2 C. onion, minced
1 (8 oz.) salmon fillets, skin removed, cut
into 1-inch pieces

## Directions

1.  Get your oven's broiler hot before doing anything else.
2.  Get a bowl, combine: pepper, egg substitute, salt, milk, and dill.
3.  Coat a frying pan with nonstick spray then begin to fry your mushrooms for 7 mins.
4.  Combine in the onion, red pepper, and potatoes.
5.  Cook the mix for 4 mins.
6.  Now add in the salmon and cook the fish for 4 mins.
7.  Top everything with the egg mix and set the heat to low.
8.  Place a lid on the pot and let the frittata cook for 8 mins.
9.  Now cook the frittata for 4 mins under the broiler.
10. Enjoy.

# Salmon & Veggie Parcel

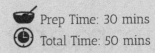

🥣 Prep Time: 30 mins

🕐 Total Time: 50 mins

Servings per Recipe: 6

| | |
|---|---|
| Calories | 226 kcal |
| Fat | 14.4 g |
| Carbohydrates | 7.1g |
| Protein | 17.3 g |
| Cholesterol | 48 mg |
| Sodium | 277 mg |

## Ingredients

6 (3-oz.) haddock fillets
Salt and freshly ground black pepper, to taste
1 yellow bell pepper, seeded and sliced thinly
1 red bell pepper, seeded and sliced thinly
4 plum tomatoes, sliced thinly
1 small onion, sliced thinly

1/2 C. fresh parsley, chopped
5 tbsps capers
1/3 C. extra-virgin olive oil
1/3 C. fresh lemon juice

## Directions

1. Set your oven to 400 degrees before doing anything else. Arrange 6 foil pieces of foil on a smooth surface. Place 1 salmon fillet on each foil.
2. Sprinkle the filet with some salt and black pepper. In a bowl, mix together the bell peppers, tomato and onion. Place the veggie mixture over each fillet evenly. Top everything with parsley and capers evenly.
3. Then drizzle the oil and lemon juice.
4. Fold the foil around the salmon mixture to seal it.
5. Arrange the foil packets onto a large baking sheet in a single layer.
6. Bake the parcels for about 20 minutes.

# SPINACH
# Summertime Steak

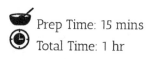 Prep Time: 15 mins
Total Time: 1 hr

Servings per Recipe: 2
Calories           494 kcal
Fat                41.5 g
Carbohydrates      6.2g
Protein            25.3 g
Cholesterol        65 mg
Sodium             7407 mg

## Ingredients

1/4 C. olive oil
2 salmon steaks
1 tbsp garlic salt, or to taste
1 tbsp onion salt, or to taste
1 tbsp paprika, or to taste
1 1/2 tsps ground black pepper, or to taste
1 1/2 tsps salt, or to taste

1 tbsp chopped chives
2 tsps chopped fresh thyme
4 leaves fresh spinach
1/4 C. Parmesan cheese

## Directions

1. Set your oven to 350 degrees F before doing anything else and lightly, coat an 8x8-inch baking dish. In a shallow dish, place oil and coat the salmon steaks with generously with more oil.

2. In another small bowl, mix together onion salt, garlic salt, paprika, salt and black pepper and season both sides of the salmon steaks with seasoning mixture.

3. Arrange the steaks into the prepared baking dish and top everything with fresh herbs, spinach and cheese.

4. Cook everything in the oven for about 45 minutes or till done completely.

# *Salmon*
# Spring Rolls with Spicy Mayo

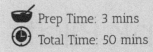 Prep Time: 3 mins

Total Time: 50 mins

Servings per Recipe: 4

| | |
|---|---|
| Calories | 507.2 |
| Cholesterol | 105.3mg |
| Sodium | 627.6mg |
| Carbohydrates | 30.7g |
| Protein | 37.2g |

## Ingredients

For Mayo:
1 C. mayonnaise
1 tbsp fresh lime juice
2 tbsps chili paste
Salt and freshly ground black pepper, to taste
For Rolls:
1 1/2 lbs boneless salmon fillets, cut into small chunks

1/4 C. fresh gingerroot, minced
1/4 C. garlic, minced
1/2 of bunch fresh cilantro, chopped
2 tbsps flour
Canola oil, as required

## Directions

1. For the mayo, in a bowl, add all the ingredients and beat till well combined and keep aside.
2. In a large bowl, mix together salmon, ginger, garlic and cilantro.
3. In a small bowl, mix together flour and enough water to form a paste.
4. Place the wrappers onto a smooth surface.
5. Divide the salmon mixture in the center of each wrapper evenly.
6. Roll the wrappers around the filling and with flour mixture, brush the edges and press to seal completely.
7. In a large cast-iron skillet or deep fryer, heat the oil to 350 degrees F.
8. Carefully, add the rolls to the skillet in batches.
9. Fry the rolls for about 3-4 minutes or till golden brown and transfer onto paper towel lined plates to drain.
10. Serve these rolls with mayo.

# PESTO
# Pink Pilaf

Prep Time: 15 mins
Total Time: 1 hr

Servings per Recipe: 4

| | |
|---|---|
| Calories | 710 kcal |
| Fat | 34.9 g |
| Carbohydrates | 44.2g |
| Protein | 44.6 g |
| Cholesterol | 122 mg |
| Sodium | 778 mg |

## Ingredients

1 1/2 lbs salmon fillets, cut into 1 inch cubes
1/3 C. pesto
2 tbsps butter
2 shallots, finely chopped

1 C. uncooked long-grain white rice
2 1/2 C. fish stock
2/3 C. dry white wine

## Directions

1. In a bowl, add salmon and pesto and toss to coat well and keep aside.
2. Melt butter in a pan on medium heat and sauté the shallots for about 2-3 minutes or till tender.
3. Add wine, broth and rice and stir to combine and bring to a boil.
4. Reduce the heat to low and simmer, covered for about 15 minutes.
5. Uncover the pan and place the salmon over rice and simmer, covered for about 25-30 minutes or till salmon and rice are done completely.

# *Pesto* Fish

Prep Time: 15 mins
Total Time: 35 mins

Servings per Recipe: 4
| | |
|---|---|
| Calories | 354 kcal |
| Fat | 25.6 g |
| Carbohydrates | 1.8g |
| Protein | 28.3 g |
| Cholesterol | 81 mg |
| Sodium | 174 mg |

## Ingredients

1/4 C. pine nuts
1/2 C. coarsely chopped fresh basil
1/4 C. grated Parmesan cheese
1 clove garlic, diced
3 tbsps extra-virgin olive oil

salt and freshly ground black pepper to taste
1 lb salmon fillet

## Directions

1. Set your grill for medium-high heat and coat the grill grate with a little cooking spray.
2. Add pine nuts in a pre-heated small nonstick skillet on medium heat and cook, stirring for about 5 minutes or till toasted.
3. In a food processor, add toasted pine nuts, Parmesan, basil and garlic and pulse till a thick paste forms.
4. While the motor is running slowly, add the oil and pulse till smooth and season with salt and black pepper.
5. Place the salmon fillets over the grill grate, skin side down and cook, covered for about 8-15 minutes or till salmon is about 2/3 done.
6. Now, place the salmon fillets onto a baking sheet and cover each fillet with pesto evenly.
7. Set your oven's broiler for heating and arrange the rack about 6 inches from the heating element.
8. Broil the salmon fillets for about 5 minutes or till the salmon is done and the pesto becomes bubbly.

# SMOKEY
# Pâté

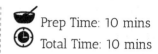
Prep Time: 10 mins
Total Time: 10 mins

Servings per Recipe: 1
Calories                1119.2
Cholesterol             372.3mg
Sodium                  943.3mg
Carbohydrates           19.5g
Protein                 65.6g

## Ingredients

1 small onion, peeled and quartered
8 oz. softened cream cheese
1 can salmon, skinned and boned
2 tbsps lemon juice
1 tbsp horseradish
2 tsps dill
1/4 C. parsley

1/2 tsp liquid smoke
1 tsp Worcestershire sauce
dash of tobasco
salt and pepper

## Directions

1.  Add the onions to the bowl of a food processer.
2.  Puree and mince the mix. Then combine in the: cream cheese, salmon, lemon juice, horseradish, dill, parsley, liquid smoke, Worcestershire, pepper, and salt.
3.  Puree the mix into a smooth paste.
4.  Now pour the mix into a bowl and place a covering of plastic on the bowl.
5.  Put everything in the fridge for 8 hrs. Enjoy.

# *Jarlsberg* and Salmon Pâté

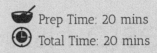

Prep Time: 20 mins
Total Time: 20 mins

Servings per Recipe: 4
Calories          454.1
Cholesterol       107.9mg
Sodium            2239.1mg
Carbohydrates     14.6g
Protein           27.9g

## Ingredients

4 oz. pate or 4 oz. liverwurst, sliced
4 cherry tomatoes, halved or 8 of the tiny tomatoes
1 large lemon
8 baby dill gherkins
1 long loaf firm bread, unsliced
4 tbsps unsalted butter
1/4 lb thinly sliced smoked salmon
1/4 lb thinly sliced cooked ham

1/4 lb jarlsberg cheese, thinly sliced
1/4 lb nokkelost cheese, thickly sliced
1/2 cucumber, scored and cut into thin slices
1 small bibb lettuce
fresh dill sprig
1 bunch watercress
1/2 small red pepper, cut in strips for garnish

## Directions

1. Divide your lemon into 2 pieces then cut one in half and slice the other pieces into thin slices.
2. Get your bread and cut it in half lengthwise then place it on a serving dish.
3. Coat each half of bread with butter.
4. Layer the following on each piece of bread: pate, lettuce leaves, salmon, gherkin, ham, tomato, cheese, lemon, and cucumber.
5. Now top everything with the pepper strips, dill, and watercress.
6. Enjoy.

# LEMON
# Pesto Fish

 Prep Time: 10 mins
Total Time: 40 mins

Servings per Recipe: 4
| | |
|---|---|
| Calories | 917 kcal |
| Fat | 67.4 g |
| Carbohydrates | 112.7g |
| Protein | 62.6 g |
| Cholesterol | 1164 mg |
| Sodium | 851 mg |

## Ingredients

2 lbs salmon fillets, de-boned
2 lemons
1 1/2 C. pesto

1/2 C. white wine

## Directions

1. Coat a baking pan with oil then lay your pieces of fish in it with the skin of the fish facing downwards.
2. Coat the fish with the juice of one freshly squeezed lemon then top everything with the wine.
3. Let the fish sit in the dish for 20 mins.
4. Now get your oven's broiler hot before doing anything else.
5. Lay your pesto over the pieces of fish evenly and cook everything under the broiler.
6. For every 1 inch of thickness in your fish. Broil it for 9 mins.
7. Now take out the fish from the oven and top them with the juice of a 2nd freshly squeezed lemon.
8. Cut the rest of the lemon into thin pieces and layer them over the fish.
9. Enjoy.

# Pink and Green
# Italian Pasta

Prep Time: 15 mins
Total Time: 40 mins

Servings per Recipe: 4

| | |
|---|---|
| Calories | 512 kcal |
| Fat | 22.6 g |
| Carbohydrates | 49.4g |
| Protein | 28.9 g |
| Cholesterol | 66 mg |
| Sodium | 1065 mg |

## Ingredients

8 oz. dry fettuccine pasta
1/4 C. butter
1 C. milk
1 tbsp all-purpose flour
1 C. freshly grated Parmesan cheese
1/2 lb smoked salmon, diced

1 C. diced fresh spinach
2 tbsps capers
1/4 C. diced sun-dried tomatoes
1/2 C. diced fresh oregano

## Directions

1. Boil your pasta in water and salt for 9 mins then remove all the liquid.
2. Begin to stir and heat your milk and butter in a large pot then once it is hot add in the flour and get everything thick.
3. Slowly add in the parmesan and continue heating it until the cheese melts.
4. Break the fish into the parmesan mix then add: the oregano, spinach, sun-dried tomatoes, and capers.
5. Let the mix simmer for 5 mins while stirring.
6. Lay your pasta on a serving plate then liberally top it with the buttery sauce. Enjoy.

# SALMON
# with Lemon
# Sauce

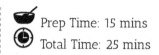 Prep Time: 15 mins

Total Time: 25 mins

Servings per Recipe: 2

| | |
|---|---|
| Calories | 1270 kc: |
| Fat | 123.7 g |
| Carbohydrates | 14.3g |
| Protein | 38.6 g |
| Cholesterol | 650 mg |
| Sodium | 21153 m; |

## Ingredients

3 tbsps fresh lemon juice
1 tbsp olive oil
Salt and pepper to taste
2 (6 oz.) skinless, boneless salmon fillets
3 egg yolks
1 tbsp hot water

1 C. butter, cut into small pieces
2 tbsps fresh lemon juice
Salt and pepper to taste
2 tbsps chopped fresh chives

## Directions

1. Get a saucepan and add in: salmon, lemon juice, pepper, olive oil, salt, and water (add enough to just cover the salmon).
2. Heat this mix until hot but not boiling.
3. Cook the salmon like this until the temperature of the fish is 140 degrees or it is opaque in color.
4. At the same time get some water boiling in a separate pan.
5. Begin to beat your yolks in a bowl and once the water is boiling add some of it to the yolks and continue mixing for a few mins.
6. Now place the bowl over the boiling water but it should not touching the water and continue whisking until the yolks have thickened.
7. You do not want to scramble the yolks. You are creating a sauce (hollandaise).
8. Now add a piece of butter and let it melt then add another until everything has been added to sauce.
9. Place the bowl to the side and add: pepper, salt, and lemon juice.
10. Top your cooked fish with the hollandaise and chives as well.
11. Enjoy.

# Quiche I (Chards and Onions)

Prep Time: 45 mins
Total Time: 1 hr 20 mins

Servings per Recipe: 8
| | |
|---|---|
| Calories | 154 kcal |
| Fat | 9.3 g |
| Carbohydrates | 6.7g |
| Protein | 10.8 g |
| Cholesterol | 99 mg |
| Sodium | 289 mg |

## Ingredients

2 tbsps butter, divided
1/4 C. plain dried bread crumbs
2 C. 2% milk
8 oz. salmon fillets, skin removed
1/3 C. chopped onion
1/2 bunch Swiss chard, chopped

1/2 tsp salt
1/8 tsp ground black pepper
1/2 tsp dried marjoram
1/8 tsp ground nutmeg
3 eggs

## Directions

1. Coat a pie dish with butter and bread crumbs. Then set your oven to 350 degrees before doing anything else. Gently boil your fish in milk.
2. Then place a lid on the pot and let the contents cook for 12 mins.
3. Now stir fry your chards and onions, in butter, in a 2nd pot, until soft, then add: nutmeg, salt, marjoram, and pepper.
4. Add the onion mix to the pie and then break up the salmon in the pie as well. Get a bowl and beat 1 C. of milk from the fish and your eggs for 1 min. Place this mix into the pie as well.
5. Cook everything in the oven for 40 mins.
6. Let the pie cool before serving. Enjoy.

# SESAME
# Orange Salmon

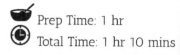 Prep Time: 1 hr

Total Time: 1 hr 10 mins

Servings per Recipe: 4
| | |
|---|---|
| Calories | 306.4 |
| Cholesterol | 87.5mg |
| Sodium | 118.4mg |
| Carbohydrates | 24.7g |
| Protein | 35.1g |

## Ingredients

1 C. thin soy sauce
2 oranges, juice of
2 oranges, zest of
3 tbsps brown sugar
4 garlic cloves
1 tbsp minced ginger

1 tbsp sesame seeds
4 (6 oz.) salmon fillets

## Directions

1.  Add the following to a pot: ginger, garlic cloves, brown sugar, orange zest, orange juice, and soy sauce.
2.  Stir the mix until it is completely smooth then get the mix boiling.
3.  Once about 1/2 of the mix has cooked out combine in the salmon and sesame seeds.
4.  Place a lid on the pot and put everything in the fridge for 2 hrs.
5.  Place the salmon on a hot grill for 4 mins each side then boil the sauce for 5 mins.
6.  When serving the salmon liberally top the fish with the sauce.
7.  Enjoy.

# Sweet Garlic
# Salmon

Prep Time: 15 mins
Total Time: 8 hrs 40 mins

Servings per Recipe: 8
| | |
|---|---|
| Calories | 384 kcal |
| Fat | 23 g |
| Carbohydrates | 11.7g |
| Protein | 31.1 g |
| Cholesterol | 83 mg |
| Sodium | 1885 mg |

## Ingredients

1 C. soy sauce
1 C. muscovado (dark brown) sugar
1 (5 inch) piece of fresh ginger root, peeled and diced
1/4 C. olive oil

2 cloves garlic, smashed
1 (3 lb) whole salmon fillet with skin
1 untreated cedar plank

## Directions

1. Get a bowl, combine evenly: garlic, soy sauce, olive oil, muscovado sugar, and garlic.
2. Get a resealable plastic bag and put your salmon in it and cover the salmon with the contents in the bowl.
3. Let the fish soak for 8 hrs in the fridge.
4. Submerge a cedar plank in water for 30 minutes before you start to grill.
5. Oil your grate and heat up the grill. Cook your salmon on the grill for 20 mins on top of the plank with the grilled covered.
6. Enjoy.

# AUTHENTIC
# Salmon Jerky

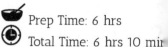

Prep Time: 6 hrs
Total Time: 6 hrs 10 min

Servings per Recipe: 24
| | |
|---|---|
| Calories | 56.0 |
| Fat | 1.6g |
| Cholesterol | 17.3mg |
| Sodium | 363.8mg |
| Carbohydrates | 1.4g |
| Protein | 8.3g |

## Ingredients

2 lbs salmon, cut into 1/4-inch thick strips
1/2 C. soy sauce
2 tbsp brown sugar
1/2 tsp fresh ginger

1/4 tsp pepper
1 tsp liquid smoke

## Directions

1. In a pan, mix together all the ingredients except salmon and bring to a boil.
2. Remove from the heat and keep aside to cool.
3. Add the salmon strips and marinate for about 15-60 minutes.
4. Set your oven to 150 degrees F.
5. Dry the salmon strips in the oven for about 5-6 hours.
6. You can preserve these strips in airtight jars.

# Buffalo
# Salmon

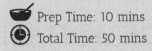 Prep Time: 10 mins

Total Time: 50 mins

Servings per Recipe: 2
| | |
|---|---|
| Calories | 496 kcal |
| Fat | 36.6 g |
| Carbohydrates | 11.3g |
| Protein | 29.5 g |
| Cholesterol | 83 mg |
| Sodium | 562 mg |

## Ingredients

1 1/2 tsps ground black pepper
1/2 tsp paprika
1/4 tsp cayenne pepper
1 tsp diced garlic
1 tbsp Dijon mustard
1 tbsp brown sugar
1/2 tsp onion powder
1/4 tsp salt

1 tbsp olive oil
2 (6 oz.) salmon fillets
2 tbsps olive oil
1 1/2 tbsps diced onion
1 tbsps sriracha

## Directions

1. Get a bowl, combine: salt, black pepper, onion powder, paprika, brown sugar, cayenne, Dijon, and diced garlic. Stir the mix until it is evenly combined. Then add in 1 tbsp of olive oil and stir everything again.

2. Coat your pieces of fish with the mix then place the fish in a casserole dish and let them sit for 40 mins with a covering of plastic on the dish.

3. Begin to stir fry your onions for 12 mins in 2 tbsps of olive oil then add in the fish and fry them for 5 mins each side. When serving the fish top them with the onions and also the oil from the pan and the sriracha.

4. Enjoy.

# CREAMY
# Salmon and Tomatoes

 Prep Time: 35 mins
Total Time: 35 mins

Servings per Recipe: 25
| | |
|---|---|
| Calories | 46 kcal |
| Fat | 3.9 g |
| Carbohydrates | 1.9g |
| Protein | < 1.4 g |
| Cholesterol | 12 mg |
| Sodium | 48 mg |

## Ingredients

50 cherry tomatoes, cleaned, dried, tops
and bottoms removed
1 (8 oz.) package cream cheese,
softened
2 oz. smoked salmon, finely chopped

2 1/2 tbsps heavy cream
3 drops lemon juice
ground black pepper to taste

## Directions

1. Take out the insides of your tomatoes and put the tomato insides in a bowl.
2. Get a 2nd bowl, combine: black pepper, cream cheese, lemon juice, salmon, and cream.
3. Use a mixer for 3 mins then add the mix to a cookie press.
4. Place the mix into the tomatoes.
5. Enjoy.

# Thai Style
# Salmon

🥣 Prep Time: 15 mins
🕐 Total Time: 15 mins

Servings per Recipe: 2
| | |
|---|---|
| Calories | 368 kcal |
| Fat | 11.6 g |
| Carbohydrates | 31g |
| Protein | 34.2 g |
| Cholesterol | 50 mg |
| Sodium | 995 mg |

## Ingredients

1 (8 oz.) can salmon, undrained
1/4 cucumber, chopped
1 tbsp capers, drained with liquid reserved and chopped
2 tbsps light mayonnaise

1 tbsp red wine vinegar
1 tsp red chili paste
1/4 tsp Sriracha
4 slices whole wheat bread, toasted

## Directions

1. Place your fish in a bowl and flake the meat.
2. Now stir everything with the liquid.
3. Add in your capers and cucumbers and stir the mix again.
4. Get a 2nd bowl, combine: chili paste, red vinegar, mayo, and the liquid from the capers.
5. Stir the mix then add in your Sriracha.
6. Now combine both bowls.
7. Evenly divide the mix between two pieces of bread then top everything with another piece of bread to form sandwiches.
8. Enjoy.

# SPICY
# Salmon

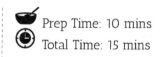 Prep Time: 10 mins

Total Time: 15 mins

Servings per Recipe: 2
| | |
|---|---|
| Calories | 271 kcal |
| Fat | 14.4 g |
| Carbohydrates | 2.5g |
| Protein | < 30.2 g |
| Cholesterol | 96 mg |
| Sodium | 605 mg |

## Ingredients

1 tsp vegetable oil
1 1/2 tbsps Dijon mustard
2 tsps rice vinegar
1/2 tsp Sriracha

salt to taste
2 (5 oz.) salmon fillets

## Directions

1. Cover a cookie sheet with foil and coat the foil with some veggie oil.
2. Get a bowl, combine: Sriracha, vinegar, and mustard.
3. Stir the mix until it is smooth then place your pieces of fish with the skin facing downwards on the sheet.
4. Liberally top them with the sauce.
5. Cook everything in the oven for 7 mins.
6. Enjoy.

# Salmon & Veggie Salad

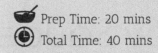

Prep Time: 20 mins
Total Time: 40 mins

Servings per Recipe: 4
| | |
|---|---|
| Calories | 1031 kcal |
| Fat | 82.1 g |
| Carbohydrates | 42.6g |
| Protein | 28.6 g |
| Cholesterol | 285 mg |
| Sodium | 3258 mg |

## Ingredients

3/4 lb chunked (not thin sliced), Alaska-style smoked salmon
1 C. bottled champagne salad dressing
sea salt and freshly ground black pepper to taste
4 oz. pickled green beans, cut in thirds
1 1/2 lbs new potatoes, red or yellow, scrubbed

3 medium tomatoes, quartered
5 eggs, hard cooked and peeled, then quartered
1/2 C. nicoise or other small, black, pitted olives

## Directions

1. In a large bowl, chop the salmon into bite-sized pieces and keep it aside.
2. In a pan of salted boiling water, cook the potatoes for about 15 minutes or till tender and drain well.
3. Now cut the potatoes into bite-sized pieces.
4. In the bowl of salmon, add the potatoes and the remaining ingredients and gently, stir to combine. Serve warm.

# GRILLED
# Soy Sauce Marinated Salmon

Prep Time: 15 mins
Total Time: 35 mins

Servings per Recipe: 6
| | |
|---|---|
| Calories | 678 kcal |
| Fat | 45.8 g |
| Carbohydrates | 1.7g |
| Protein | 61.3 g |
| Cholesterol | 179 mg |
| Sodium | 981 mg |

## Ingredients

3 (12 inch) untreated cedar planks
1/3 C. vegetable oil
1 1/2 tbsps rice vinegar
1 tsp sesame oil
1/3 C. soy sauce

1/4 C. chopped green onions
1 tbsp grated fresh ginger root
1 tsp diced garlic
2 (2 lb) salmon fillets, skin removed

## Directions

1. Set your outdoor grill for medium heat and coat the grill grate lightly.
2. In a bowl of warm water, soak the cedar planks for about 1 hour.
3. In a large bowl, mix together both oils, vinegar, soy sauce, green onion, garlic and ginger and coat the salmon fillets with the mixture generously.
4. Cover and keep aside for about 15-60 minutes.
5. Arrange the planks onto the grill grate.
6. The boards are ready when they just start to crackle and smoke.
7. Remove the salmon fillets from the bowl and discard the marinade and arrange on the planks.
8. Cook everything on the grill, covered for about 20 minutes or till done completely.

# *Salmon* Corn & Veggie Bisque

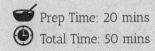

Prep Time: 20 mins
Total Time: 50 mins

Servings per Recipe: 6
Calories             295.4
Cholesterol          50.8mg
Sodium               203.5mg
Carbohydrates        30.9g
Protein              23.7g

## Ingredients

1 lb fresh salmon fillet, skin removed, bones removed
1 tbsp cooking oil
2 C. chopped carrots
1 C. chopped onion
1/2 C. chopped red pepper
1/2 C. chopped celery
1 1/2 C. water

4 C. low sodium chicken broth
2 1/2 C. cubed red potatoes
1 C. corn kernel
2 C. milk
2 tbsps cornstarch
2 tsps dill
1 pinch salt, to taste

## Directions

1. Rinse the salmon and with a paper towel, pat dry it completely.
2. Heat oil in a large pan on medium-high heat and sauté onion, celery, pepper and carrots for about 10 minutes or till all the vegetables become tender.
3. In another pan of boiling water, add the salmon and bring to a boil again.
4. Reduce the heat to low and simmer, covered for about 6-8 minutes or till done.
5. Drain the salmon well then cut it into 1/2-inch pieces.
6. Add corn, potatoes, dill, broth and salt into the pan with the vegetables and bring to a boil.
7. Reduce the heat to medium-low, cover and simmer, stirring occasionally for about 15 minutes or till the potatoes are done.
8. Meanwhile in a bowl, mix together the cornstarch and 1/2 C. of milk and add into the soup, stirring continuously.
9. Stir in the remaining milk and cook on medium heat for about 2 minutes,
10. Carefully, add the salmon and cook till heated completely.

# SALAD
# In Seattle

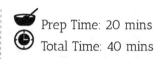 Prep Time: 20 mins

Total Time: 40 mins

Servings per Recipe: 4
| | |
|---|---|
| Calories | 1031 kca |
| Fat | 82.1 g |
| Carbohydrates | 42.6g |
| Protein | 28.6 g |
| Cholesterol | 285 mg |
| Sodium | 3258 mg |

## Ingredients

3/4 lb chunked (not thin sliced), Alaska-style smoked salmon
1 C. bottled champagne salad dressing
sea salt and freshly ground black pepper to taste
4 oz. pickled green beans, cut in thirds
1 1/2 lbs new potatoes, red or yellow, scrubbed

3 medium tomatoes, quartered
5 eggs, hard cooked and peeled, then quartered
1/2 C. nicoise or other small, black, pitted olives

## Directions

1.  In a large bowl, chop the salmon into bite-sized pieces and keep it aside.
2.  In a pan of salted boiling water, cook the potatoes for about 15 minutes or till tender and drain well.
3.  Now cut the potatoes into bite-sized pieces.
4.  In the bowl of salmon, add the potatoes and the remaining ingredients and gently, stir to combine.
5.  Serve warm.

# *Salmon* Stew (Abalos Style)

Prep Time: 10 mins
Total Time: 25 mins

Servings per Recipe: 4

| | |
|---|---|
| Calories | 223 kcal |
| Carbohydrates | 4.8 g |
| Cholesterol | 45 mg |
| Fat | 11 g |
| Protein | 24.9 g |
| Sodium | 466 mg |

## Ingredients

1 tbsp olive oil
4 cloves garlic, minced
1 onion, diced
1 tomato, diced
1 (14.75 ounce) can pink salmon
2 1/2 cups water

bay leaf (optional)
salt and ground black pepper to taste
1 tsp fish sauce (optional)

## Directions

1. Cook onion and garlic in hot oil for about 5 minutes before adding tomato and salmon into it.

2. Cook for another 3 minutes and then add water, fish sauce, bay leaf, salt and pepper.

3. Cover the skillet and cook for 20 minutes.

4. Serve.

# MOROCCAN
# Salmon Cake

 Prep Time: 20 mins

Total Time: 45 mins

Servings per Recipe: 4

| | |
|---|---|
| Calories | 620 kcal |
| Fat | 46.4 g |
| Carbohydrates | 26.4g |
| Protein | 28.8 g |
| Cholesterol | 178 mg |
| Sodium | 950 mg |

## Ingredients

Mayo Topping:
1/2 C. mayonnaise
1 clove garlic, crushed
1/8 tsp paprika
Salmon Cake:
1/2 C. couscous
2/3 C. orange juice
1 (14.75 oz.) can red salmon, drained
1 (10 oz.) package frozen chopped
spinach, thawed, drained and squeezed
dry

2 egg yolks, beaten
2 cloves garlic, crushed
1 tsp ground cumin
1/2 tsp ground black pepper
1/2 tsp salt
3 tbsps olive oil

## Directions

1. Get a bowl, mix: paprika, mayo, and garlic.
2. Boil your orange juice in a large pot, then add in your couscous.
3. Get the mix boiling again and then place a lid on the pot, shut the heat, and let the couscous stand for 7 mins.
4. Now stir your couscous after it has lost all of its heat.
5. Get a 2nd bowl, combine: salt, salmon, black pepper, spinach, cumin, egg yolks, and garlic.
6. Shape this mix into patties and then fry them in olive oil for 8 mins turning each at 4 mins.
7. When serving add a topping of mayo.
8. Enjoy.

# *Sweet*
# Salmon Stir Fry

🥣 Prep Time: 15 mins
🕐 Total Time: 55 mins

Servings per Recipe: 4
| | |
|---|---|
| Calories | 523 kcal |
| Fat | 30.4 g |
| Carbohydrates | 20.3g |
| Protein | 41 g |
| Cholesterol | 127 mg |
| Sodium | 399 mg |

## Ingredients

4 leeks
2 tbsps butter
1 tbsp brown sugar
3 carrots, cut into matchsticks
kosher salt to taste
2 lbs salmon fillets

2 tsps olive oil
kosher salt and ground black pepper to taste

## Directions

1. Cover a casserole dish with foil and nonstick spray then set your oven to 425 degrees before doing anything else.
2. Chop up your leeks removing the hard leaves, and the root.
3. Now rinse the leeks under cold water and pat them dry.
4. Stir fry the leeks in butter for 7 mins. Then add brown sugar and continue cooking for 17 more mins (low to medium heat stir in intervals of 4 mins).
5. Add: salt and carrots.
6. Cook everything for 7 more mins.
7. Layer your salmon in the casserole dish and top the fish with olive oil, pepper, and salt.
8. Cook the salmon in the oven for 9 to 12 mins for each side.
9. Place everything on serving plates and evenly divide the leeks amongst our salmon servings.
10. Enjoy.

# CILANTRO
# Salmon Spaghetti

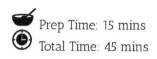

Prep Time: 15 mins
Total Time: 45 mins

| Servings per Recipe: 2 | |
|---|---|
| Calories | 896 kcal |
| Fat | 56.7 g |
| Carbohydrates | 62.2g |
| Protein | 31.3 g |
| Cholesterol | 216 mg |
| Sodium | 401 mg |

## Ingredients

1/2 (8 oz.) package spaghetti
1 tbsp butter
1 large leek - light parts only, rinsed,
and diced
salt to taste
1/2 C. white wine
1/2 lemon, juiced

1 C. crème fraiche
1 tsp tarragon Dijon mustard
1 pinch cayenne pepper, or to taste
6 oz. skinless, boneless salmon, sliced
1/2 C. diced cilantro, or to taste
1 pinch cayenne pepper

## Directions

1. Boil your pasta in water and salt for 13 mins then remove all the liquid.
2. Stir fry your leeks in butter for 8 mins then add in salt, lemon juice, and wine.
3. Get everything boiling and let the contents gently cook for 7 mins until most of the liquid has cooked out.
4. Now add your crème, cayenne, and mustard.
5. Lower the heat and continue cooking the contents for 6 mins then add your fish and cook the fish for 4 more mins.
6. Shut the heat and add the cilantro.
7. Combine the salmon and sauce with the pasta and stir everything.
8. When serving the dish add a bit more cayenne.
9. Enjoy.

# Swiss Chard, Salmon and Quinoa

Prep Time: 15 mins
Total Time: 1 hr

Servings per Recipe: 4
Calories            471 kcal
Fat                 18 g
Carbohydrates       40.1g
Protein             26.2 g
Cholesterol         38 mg
Sodium              402 mg

## Ingredients

2 tbsps olive oil
1 onion, diced
2 cloves garlic, minced
1 C. uncooked quinoa
2 C. vegetable broth
3/4 lb salmon fillets
1 C. white wine
1/2 C. water, or more as needed to cover
1 tbsp olive oil
2 cloves garlic, minced

1 bunch Swiss chard, stems and tough ribs
removed, leaves cut into 1/2-inch-wide
ribbons
2 tbsps lemon juice
salt to taste
1 pinch ground black pepper

## Directions

1. Stir fry 2 cloves of garlic and the onions in 2 tbsps of olive oil for 4 mins.
2. Add the quinoa and toast it for 6 more mins before adding in the broth.
3. Get everything boiling and then place a lid on the pot. Set the heat to low and cook the quinoa for 22 mins.
4. At the same time begin to gently boil your salmon in wine for 14 mins with a low to medium level of heat.
5. Remove the salmon from the pan and let it cool before flaking it and taking off the skins.
6. For 2 mins, stir fry 2 more pieces of garlic in 1 tbsp of olive oil then add the lemon juice and the chards.
7. Fry the chards for 3 mins then place everything to the side.
8. Add the salmon flakes to the quinoa and mix it all together then add the chards and mix again.
9. Top the quinoa with pepper and salt.
10. Enjoy.

# WRAPPED
# Salmon

Prep Time: 20 mins
Total Time: 45 mins

Servings per Recipe: 2

| | |
|---|---|
| Calories | 605 kcal |
| Fat | 33.1 g |
| Carbohydrates | 20.2g |
| Protein | 56.6 g |
| Cholesterol | 1141 mg |
| Sodium | 755 mg |

## Ingredients

6 slices bacon, cut crosswise into 1/2-inch pieces
2 ears white corn
1/4 C. chopped green onions - white and light green parts separated from green tops
1/4 C. diced red bell pepper
salt and ground black pepper to taste
1 pinch cayenne pepper, or to taste
2 tsps olive oil
1 tbsp rice vinegar, or more to taste

1/2 tsp vegetable oil
2 (8 oz.) center-cut boneless salmon fillets
1 pinch cayenne pepper, or to taste
1 C. fresh spinach leaves (optional)

## Directions

1. Get your grill hot and coat the grate with oil.
2. Now cut the kernels off the ears into a bowl before doing anything else.
3. Fry your bacon for 9 mins.
4. Then add in: bell peppers and green onions. Cook for 3 mins before adding: vinegar, salt, olive oil, black pepper, onion tops, and cayenne.
5. Now shut the heat.
6. Coat your pieces of salmon with veggie oil, cayenne, pepper, and salt.
7. For 6 mins per side grill the salmon.
8. Plate your salmon then layer the bacon mix and spinach on top.
9. Enjoy.

# Spinach and Pesto Puff Pastry

Prep Time: 15 mins
Total Time: 35 mins

Servings per Recipe: 24
| | |
|---|---|
| Calories | 685 kcal |
| Carbohydrates | 38.9 g |
| Cholesterol | 55 mg |
| Fat | 43.7 g |
| Protein | 33.5 g |
| Sodium | 529 mg |

## Ingredients

2 (12 oz) skinless, boneless salmon fillets
seasoned salt to taste
1/2 tsp garlic powder
1 tsp onion powder
1 (17.25 oz) package frozen puff pastry, thawed

1/3 C. pesto
1 (6 oz) package spinach leaves

## Directions

1. Set your oven at 375 degrees F before doing anything else.
2. Coat salmon with a mixture of salt, onion powder and garlic powder before setting it aside.
3. Now place ½ of your spinach between two separate puff pastry sheets, while putting more in the center and place salmon fillet over each one in the center before placing pesto and remaining spinach.
4. Moisten up the edges with water and fold it.
5. Bake this in the preheated oven for about 25 minutes.
6. Cool it down.
7. Serve.

# ENGLISH
# Fish Savory Pie of Salmon and Haddock

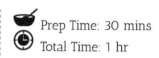

Prep Time: 30 mins
Total Time: 1 hr

Servings per Recipe: 4
| | |
|---|---|
| Calories | 695 kcal |
| Fat | 26.4 g |
| Carbohydrates | 58.8g |
| Protein | 55 g |
| Cholesterol | 148 mg |
| Sodium | 1332 mg |

## Ingredients

1 tbsp olive oil
2 onions, halved and sliced
6 potatoes, peeled and cubed
2 C. frozen green peas
2 (6 oz.) salmon fillets, cut into 1 inch cubes
1 lb smoked haddock fillets, undyed, cut into 1 inch cubes
1 C. flaked or diced smoked salmon

1 tbsp butter
1 tbsp all-purpose flour
3 C. milk
1 1/2 C. Red Leicester cheese, grated
1 tsp ground nutmeg
1 tsp ground black pepper, or to taste
1/2 tsp salt

## Directions

1. Coat a casserole dish with oil and then set your oven to 350 degrees before doing anything else.
2. Stir fry your onions for 10 mins in oil.
3. Boil your potatoes until soft in a separate pot. Then remove all the liquid and place the potatoes in a casserole dish.
4. Put the following in the dish as well: smoked salmon, onions, haddock, and regular salmon.
5. Now add some butter and flour to the same pot that the onions were fried in.
6. Cook and stir the contents to make a roux then add in your milk and get the contents lightly boiling. Stir and simmer until everything gets thick.
7. Finally add in your pepper, salt, and nutmeg. Add your cheese and stir until melted. Save a bit of cheese for a garnish later.
8. Cover your salmon with the new sauce. And add your remaining cheese.
9. Cook everything in the oven for 33 mins.
10. Enjoy.

# Restaurant Style
# Linguine

🍲 Prep Time: 10 mins
🕐 Total Time: 20 mins

Servings per Recipe: 4
| | |
|---|---|
| Calories | 583 kcal |
| Carbohydrates | 64.4 g |
| Cholesterol | 205 mg |
| Fat | 27.1 g |
| Protein | 21 g |
| Sodium | 373 mg |

## Ingredients

2 (8 oz) packages fresh linguine pasta
1 C. cream
4 oz smoked salmon, chopped
1 pinch freshly grated nutmeg (optional)
1 pinch ground black pepper, or to taste
(optional)

1 1/2 tbsps black caviar
1 bunch chopped flat leaf parsley

## Directions

1. Boil your pasta in water and salt for 7 to 10 mins until al dente. Drain the liquid and set aside.
2. Get a saucepan and heat up your cream, then cook your salmon with pepper and nutmeg. Coat the pasta with this mixture. Add caviar as well.
3. Garnish everything with some parsley.
4. Enjoy.

# PAELLA
# in Tunisian Style

Prep Time: 35 mins
Total Time: 1 hr 3 mins

Servings per Recipe: 6

| | |
|---|---|
| Calories | 519 |
| Fat | 16.8 |
| Cholesterol | 76 |
| Sodium | 707 |
| Carbohydrates | 55.8 |
| Protein | 30.3 |

## Ingredients

1/4 C. olive oil
1 onion, chopped
1 roasted red pepper, chopped
2 cloves garlic, chopped
3 vine-ripened tomatoes, chopped
1 (8 ounce) salmon fillet, cut into pieces
5 ounces beef sausage, cut into pieces
6 C. vegetable broth, divided
1/2 C. white wine

1 tsp. ground cumin
salt and ground black pepper
12 shrimp, shelled and deveined
12 mussels, cleaned and debearded
2 (5.8 ounce) boxes couscous

## Directions

1. Pour olive oil into a skillet and heat well. Sauté onion, garlic and roasted red pepper and leave for 5 minutes.

2. Add tomatoes, salmon and sausage and cook for 4 minutes.

3. Stir in 2 1/2 C. of broth and white wine into the skillet. Add salt, pepper and cumin and allow the mixture to boil.

4. Lower the heat and add the shrimp and leave for 4 minutes until the shrimp becomes pink. Transfer from heat, add the mussels and leave for about 6 minutes until the mussels open fully.

5. Pour the balance 3 1/2 C. of broth to a separate saucepan and allow to boil. Add couscous and combine well. Transfer from heat and leave for 6 minutes until the couscous absorbs the liquid.

6. Dish out couscous into bowls; drizzle the stew mixture on top.

7. Enjoy.

# A Quiche
# from Maine

Prep Time: 45 mins
Total Time: 1 hr 20 mins

Servings per Recipe: 8
| | |
|---|---|
| Calories | 154 kcal |
| Fat | 9.3 g |
| Carbohydrates | 6.7g |
| Protein | 10.8 g |
| Cholesterol | 99 mg |
| Sodium | 289 mg |

## Ingredients

2 tbsps butter, divided
1/4 C. plain dried bread crumbs
2 C. 2% milk
8 oz. salmon fillets, skin removed
1/3 C. diced onion
1/2 bunch Swiss chard, diced

1/2 tsp salt
1/8 tsp ground black pepper
1/2 tsp dried marjoram
1/8 tsp ground nutmeg
3 eggs

## Directions

1. Coat a pie dish with 1 tbsp of butter then set your oven to 350 degrees before doing anything else.
2. Now coat the pie dish with bread crumbs and shake off any excess.
3. Begin to simmer your salmon in milk, in a large pot with a lid.
4. Cook the salmon for 12 mins.
5. Now in a separate pan begin to stir fry your chards and onions in the rest of the butter.
6. Once all of the liquid has cooked out add: nutmeg, salt, marjoram, and pepper.
7. Remove everything from the pan and let the contents cool.
8. Enter the onion mix in to the pie dish and then flake your salmon into the mix as well.
9. Now get a bowl, combine: 1 C. of milk from the salmon and the eggs.
10. Pour this into the pie crust as well and cook everything in the oven for 40 mins.
11. Enjoy.

# GLAZED
# Salmon Fillets with Orzo

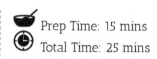

Prep Time: 15 mins
Total Time: 25 mins

Servings per Recipe: 4
| | |
|---|---|
| Calories | 849.7 |
| Fat | 31.3g |
| Cholesterol | 153.6mg |
| Sodium | 3001.4m |
| Carbohydrates | 55.8g |
| Protein | 81.8g |

## Ingredients

4 salmon fillets ( 2 lbs
1 oz. canola oil
1 oz. soy sauce
8 oz. teriyaki sauce
8 oz. orzo pasta, precooked
2 garlic cloves, minced
2 tbsp olive oil, combined with garlic

1/2 C. red bell pepper, diced
1/3 C. parmesan cheese
8 oz. spinach, julienned

## Directions

1.  Before you do anything preheat the grill and grease it.
2.  Coat the salmon fillets with soy sauce and brush them with the oil. Cook them in the grill for 4 min on each side.
3.  Brush the salmon fillets with 2 oz. of teriyaki glaze. Cook them for 3 min on each side.
4.  Cook the orzo according to the directions on the package.
5.  Place a large wok over medium heat. Heat the oil in it. Add the garlic with peppers and orzo. Cook them for 2 min.
6.  Stir in the cheese until it melts. Turn off the heat and add the spinach. Stir them several times until the spinach wilts.
7.  Serve your orzo with the glazed salmon fillets and the remaining teriyaki sauce.
8.  Enjoy.

# *Spicy*
# Salmon Fillets

🥣 Prep Time: 10 mins
🕐 Total Time: 20 mins

Servings per Recipe: 2
| | |
|---|---|
| Calories | 87.3 |
| Fat | 3.8g |
| Cholesterol | 25.8mg |
| Sodium | 121.4mg |
| Carbohydrates | 1.1g |
| Protein | 11.7g |

## Ingredients

2 tbsp cilantro leaves, chopped
1 tsp paprika
1 tsp fresh lemon juice
1/2 tsp garlic, minced
1/2 tsp extra virgin olive oil
1/4 tsp cumin

1 pinch dried red chili pepper, crushed
1 pinch salt
4 oz salmon fillets (skinless)
Olive oil flavored cooking spray

## Directions

1. Get a mixing bowl: mix in it all the ingredients except for the salmon.
2. Place the mix to the salmon fillets and place them in a mixing bowl. Cover it with a piece of plastic and place it in the fridge for 1 h.
3. Place a large skillet over medium heat. Heat a splash of oil in it. Add the salmon fillets and cook them for 3 min on each side. Serve them warm.
4. Enjoy.

# CONNECTICUT
# Brunch Sandwiches

Prep Time: 15 mins
Total Time: 35 mins

Servings per Recipe: 2

| | |
|---|---|
| Calories | 567.6 |
| Fat | 43.8g |
| Cholesterol | 302.4mg |
| Sodium | 710.4mg |
| Carbohydrates | 26.7g |
| Protein | 16.8g |

## Ingredients

2 croissants, halved horizontally
4 tbsp butter
2 eggs
salt and pepper
1 tbsp heavy cream

2 oz. smoked salmon, chopped
1 sprig dill

## Directions

1. Set your oven to 350 degrees F before doing anything else.
2. Arrange the croissant halves onto a baking sheet and cook in the oven for about 5-6 minutes.
3. Meanwhile, in a bowl, add the eggs, salt and pepper and beat well.
4. In a frying pan, add the butter over low heat and cook until melted.
5. Add the eggs and cook for about 2 minutes, mixing continuously.
6. Remove from the heat and stir in the salmon and cream until well combined.
7. Place the salmon mixture into each croissant and enjoy with a garnishing of the dill.

# *European*
# Grilled Cheese

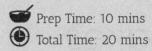 Prep Time: 10 mins

Total Time: 20 mins

Servings per Recipe: 4
| | |
|---|---|
| Calories | 352.1 |
| Fat | 15.2g |
| Cholesterol | 54.0mg |
| Sodium | 1013.0mg |
| Carbohydrates | 31.2g |
| Protein | 22.3g |

## Ingredients

8 slices pumpernickel bread
6 1/2 oz. havarti cheese, sliced
4 oz. smoked salmon

1 tbsp chopped dill

## Directions

1. Place the cheese onto 4 bread slices, followed by the salmon and dill.
2. Cover each with the remaining bread slices.
3. Place a skillet over medium-low heat until heated through.
4. Add the sandwiches and cook for about 10 minutes, flipping once halfway through.

# FISH
# Cakes

Prep Time: 15 mins
Total Time: 35 mins

Servings per Recipe: 4
| | |
|---|---|
| Calories | 263.1 |
| Fat | 10.2g |
| Cholesterol | 135.1mg |
| Sodium | 516.5mg |
| Carbohydrates | 15.4g |
| Protein | 27.3g |

## Ingredients

1 (14 3/4 oz.) canned salmon
1/4 C. onion, finely chopped
1/4 C. cornmeal
1/4 C. flour

1 egg
3 tbsp mayonnaise

## Directions

1. Open the can of the salmon and drain completely.
2. In a bowl, place the salmon and with a fork, flake evenly.
3. Add onion, cornmeal, flour, mayonnaise and egg and mix till well combined.
4. Make equal sized patties from the mixture.
5. In a skillet, heat the oil on medium heat and cook the patties till browned from both sides.

# West Indian
# Ceviche

🍲 Prep Time: 40 mins
🕐 Total Time: 42 mins

Servings per Recipe: 4
Calories            470.4
Fat                 13.0g
Cholesterol         265.0mg
Sodium              1131.5mg
Carbohydrates       61.3g
Protein             42.5g

## Ingredients

1/2 lb. salmon, cubed
1 lb. of shell-less shrimp
1 big mango, peeled and diced
1/2 red onion, diced
4 small tomatoes, peeled and diced
1 chile serrano pepper, chopped

cilantro, to desire
1 avocado, diced
20 limes, juice

## Directions

1. Get a mixing bowl: Stir in it the shrimp and salmon with lime juice. Season them with a pinch of salt.

2. Cover the bowl and place it in the fridge for 2 h 30 min.

3. Once the time is up, drain the shrimp and salmon. Transfer them to another mixing bowl.

4. Add the remaining ingredients and toss them to coat.

5. Spoon your ceviche into serving glasses and serve them.

6. Enjoy.

# ISABELLE'S
# Ceviche

Prep Time: 3 hrs
Total Time: 3 hrs

Servings per Recipe: 4
| | |
|---|---|
| Calories | 341.7 |
| Fat | 4.9g |
| Cholesterol | 179.5mg |
| Sodium | 290.3mg |
| Carbohydrates | 30.3g |
| Protein | 44.8g |

## Ingredients

2/3 lb. large shrimp, peeled and cleaned
2/3 lb. scallops, quartered
2/3 lb. salmon, skinned and pin-boned
1 tomatoes, chopped
1 mango, peeled and cubed
1/4 red onion, chopped
1 jalapeno, seeded and
1 C. lime juice
2/3 C. orange juice

1/2 C. loosely packed coriander leaves, chopped
1 tbsp powdered sugar
1 large oranges, peeled and segmented
popcorn, seasoned with chili, cumin, and salt

## Directions

1. Bring a salted saucepan of water to a boil. Cook in it the shrimp for 1 min.
2. Drain it and transfer it to an ice bowl of water. Drain it again and transfer it to a mixing bowl.
3. Add to them the scallops with salmon, mango, onion, chile, lime and orange juice.
4. Cover the bowl and place it in the fridge for 3 h 30 min.
5. Once the time is up, drain the fish and transfer it to a mixing bowl.
6. Stir into them coriander, sugar, orange, and a pinch of salt. Serve your ceviche right away.
7. Enjoy.

# Salmon
# Tenders

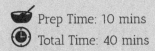 Prep Time: 10 mins

Total Time: 40 mins

Servings per Recipe: 4

| | |
|---|---|
| Calories | 436.3 |
| Fat | 26.9g |
| Cholesterol | 96.8mg |
| Sodium | 787.0mg |
| Carbohydrates | 14.2g |
| Protein | 33.8g |

## Ingredients

1 lb. salmon fillet, cut into pieces
1/4 C. chopped onion
1 - 2 clove garlic
3/4 C. mayonnaise
1/2 tsp lemon pepper

1/2 C. milk
1 C. grated Parmesan cheese

## Directions

1. Set your oven to 350 degrees F before doing anything else and lightly, grease a 13x9 - inch baking dish.

2. In a blender, add the mayo, onion, garlic and lemon pepper and pulse until well combined.

3. In 3 different shallow bowls, place, milk, mayo mixture and cheese respectively.

4. Dip each salmon piece in the milk, then in the mayo mixture and finally coat with the cheese.

5. In the prepared baking dish, arrange the salmon pieces, skin side down and top with the remaining cheese.

6. Cook in the oven for about 30 minutes.

7. Enjoy hot.

# CALIFORNIA
# Sushi Salad II

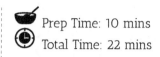 Prep Time: 10 mins

Total Time: 22 mins

Servings per Recipe: 4

| | |
|---|---|
| Calories | 507.4 |
| Fat | 15.0g |
| Cholesterol | 52.3mg |
| Sodium | 341.9mg |
| Carbohydrates | 62.2g |
| Protein | 30.0g |

## Ingredients

1 lb. frozen skinless salmon fillet, thawed
salt and pepper
1/4 C. rice vinegar
1 tbsp soy sauce
1 tsp sugar
1 tsp sesame oil

4 C. cooked short-grain rice
1 cucumber, seeded and sliced
1 avocado, pitted, peeled, and sliced
1 tbsp toasted white sesame seeds

## Directions

1. Set your grill for medium heat and lightly, grease the grill grate.
2. Sprinkle the salmon fillet with the salt and pepper evenly.
3. Cook the salmon on the grill for about 4 minutes per side.
4. Remove from the grill and place the salmon fillet onto a cutting board to cool slightly
5. After cooling, break the salmon into chunks.
6. Meanwhile, in a bowl, add the sugar, soy sauce, vinegar and sesame oil and beat until the sugar is dissolved.
7. Divide the rice into 4 bowls, followed by the salmon, cucumber, avocado and dressing.
8. Enjoy with a topping of the sesame seeds.

# *Zucchini*
# Seafood Salad

Prep Time: 18 mins
Total Time: 28 mins

Servings per Recipe: 4
| | |
|---|---|
| Calories | 478.7 |
| Fat | 13.2 g |
| Cholesterol | 52.1 mg |
| Sodium | 563.8 mg |
| Carbohydrates | 53.0 g |
| Protein | 34.8 g |

## Ingredients

1 1/3 C. couscous
2 1/3 C. chicken broth
1 small garlic clove, minced
3 medium carrots, peeled and shredded
1/2 lb. tomatoes, chopped
1 small zucchini, thinly sliced
1/4 C. fresh cilantro, chopped

1 tbsp. fresh mint leaves, make into tight bundle and slice very finely
2 tbsp. olive oil
1 lb. salmon
salt and pepper, to taste
lemon wedge

## Directions

1. Place a pot over high heat. Heat in it the broth until it starts boiling.
2. Stir in the couscous and turn off the heat. Put on the lid and let it sit for 12 min.
3. Stir in the garlic with carrot, tomatoes, zucchini, cilantro, mint, olive oil, a pinch of salt and pepper.
4. Before you do anything else, preheat the grill and grease it.
5. Coat the salmon with a cooking spray or some oil. Season it with a pinch of salt and pepper.
6. Grill it for 5 to 6 min on each side. Serve it warm with the couscous salad.
7. Enjoy.

# EGGS
# in a Boat II
# (Country Style)

Prep Time: 5 mins
Total Time: 10 mins

Servings per Recipe: 2

| | |
|---|---|
| Calories | 488.4 |
| Fat | 25.3g |
| Cholesterol | 255.8mg |
| Sodium | 1011.5mg |
| Carbohydrates | 39.1g |
| Protein | 25.7g |

## Ingredients

2 slices country bread
1 tbsp. unsalted butter
2 large eggs
1/4 cup crème fraiche
4 ounces smoked salmon

1 tbsp. capers
1/2 small red onion, sliced
black pepper

## Directions

1.  Cut a hole of about 3" diameter with the use of a drinking glass on each bread slice. Place the butter in a frying pan and allow to melt. Place the slices of bread in the frying pan, break and egg into the hole.

2.  Sprinkle salmon, capers, crème fraiche and red onion on top; adjust seasonings with about 1/4 tsp pepper.

3.  Enjoy.

# *Roasted*
# Seafood Basmati

Prep Time: 30 mins
Total Time: 1 hr

| Servings per Recipe: 4 | |
| --- | --- |
| Calories | 405.7 |
| Fat | 18.6g |
| Cholesterol | 54.7mg |
| Sodium | 865.8mg |
| Carbohydrates | 33.8g |
| Protein | 25.0g |

## Ingredients

1 (12 oz.) bag Baby Spinach
3 C. cooked basmati rice
1 tsp salt
1 tsp black pepper
3 green onions, chopped
1 tsp unsalted butter
2 tbsp extra virgin olive oil
1 C. fat free sour cream
1/2 C. light mayonnaise

1/4 C. Egg Beaters egg substitute
1/2 C. grated Parmesan cheese
2 tbsp Dijon mustard
1 lb. salmon fillet
nonstick cooking spray

## Directions

1. Set your oven to 350 degrees F before doing anything else and grease a large baking dish with cooking spray.
2. In a large skillet, heat the oil and butter over medium heat and sauté the onion and garlic until tender.
3. Stir in the spinach and cook until spinach is wilted.
4. In a large bowl, add the mayo, sour cream, mustard, 1/4 C. of the Parmesan cheese, salt and pepper and mix until well combined.
5. In a small bowl, reserve 1/2 C. of the sour cream mixture.
6. In the bowl of the remaining sour cream mixture, add the rice, spinach mixture and egg beaters and mix until well combined.
7. Place he mixture into the prepared baking dish wand top with the salmon, followed by the reserved sour cream mixture and remaining cheese.
8. Cook in the oven for about 25-30 minutes.

# ALASKAN
# Layered Crepes

Prep Time: 15 mins
Total Time: 1 hr 15 mins

Servings per Recipe: 24
| | |
|---|---|
| Calories | 116.6 |
| Fat | 8.3g |
| Cholesterol | 48.0mg |
| Sodium | 207.5mg |
| Carbohydrates | 5.8g |
| Protein | 4.5g |

## Ingredients

Crepes
1 C. flour
3 eggs
1 tsp. salt
1 1/2 C. milk
3 tbsp. butter, melted and cooled
Seafood Layer
1 (7 oz.) cans salmon, boneless skinless
1/4 C. mayonnaise

1 tbsp. chopped chives
pepper
Cheese Layer
6 oz. cream cheese, softened
2 tbsp. mayonnaise
4 slices turkey bacon, cooked crumbled

## Directions

1. For the crepes: in a bowl, add the flour and salt and mix well.
2. Add the butter, eggs and milk and with a hand mixer, beat until very smooth.
3. Keep aside for about 30 minutes.
4. Place a lightly greased crepe pan over medium heat until heated through.
5. Place desired amount of the mixture and tilt the pan to spread in a thin layer.
6. Cook until golden brown from both sides.
7. Repeat with the remaining mixture.
8. Keep the all 14 cooked crepes aside to cool completely.
9. After cooling, trim each crepe into a 6-inch diameter.
10. For the salmon layer: in a bowl, add the salmon, chives, 1/4 C. of the mayonnaise and pepper and with a fork, mash until well combined and smooth.
11. For the cream cheese layer: in a bowl, add the cream cheese, 2 tbsp. of the mayonnaise and bacon and mix until smooth.
12. Arrange 2 crepes onto a cutting board.

13. Place about 1/6 of the salmon mixture onto each crepe evenly.
14. Place another 2 crepes over the salmon mixture.
15. Place about 1/6 of the cream cheese over the crepes.
16. Repeat the layers in the same way to have two stacks.
17. With a plastic wrap, wrap each stack and place in the fridge for about 1 1/2 hours.
18. Cut each stack into 12 equal sized wedges and enjoy.

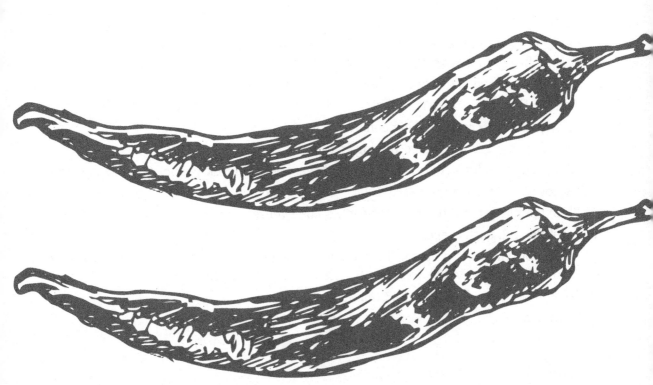

# NEW HAMPSHIRE
# Salmon Crepes

Prep Time: 20 mins
Total Time: 30 mins

| Servings per Recipe: 4 | |
| --- | --- |
| Calories | 281.2 |
| Fat | 23.4g |
| Cholesterol | 222.9mg |
| Sodium | 512.8mg |
| Carbohydrates | 4.7g |
| Protein | 13.1g |

## Ingredients

1 tbsp. chopped onion
2 tbsp. butter
1 tbsp. flour
1 C. light cream
4 oz. smoked salmon, diced
3 hard-cooked eggs, chopped
2 tbsp. capers

1/2 tsp. chopped fresh dill
1/2 tsp. fresh lemon juice
salt and black pepper
8 warm crepes
2 tbsp. grated Parmesan cheese

## Directions

1. Set your oven to 400 degrees F before doing anything else and grease a baking dish.
2. For the filling: in a wok, add 1 tbsp. of the butter and cook until melted.
3. Add the onion and stir fry for about 4-5 minutes.
4. Add the flour and stir to combine.
5. Slowly, add the cream, mixing continuously.
6. Cook for about 3-4 minutes, mixing frequently.
7. Add the eggs, salmon, dill, capers, lemon juice, salt and black pepper and stir to combine.
8. Remove from the heat.
9. Place the filling onto the center of each crepe evenly.
10. Carefully, roll each crepe.
11. In the bottom of the prepared baking dish, arrange the rolled crepes and top with the Parmesan cheese evenly, followed by the butter in the shape of dots.
12. Cook in the oven for about 5-8 minutes.
13. Enjoy warm.

# *Japanese*
# Spring Roll Wraps

🥣 Prep Time: 20 mins
🕐 Total Time: 25 mins

Servings per Recipe: 1
| | |
|---|---|
| Calories | 187.8 |
| Fat | 9.1g |
| Cholesterol | 23.0mg |
| Sodium | 2054.0mg |
| Carbohydrates | 4.9g |
| Protein | 22.0g |

## Ingredients

4 rice paper sheets
25 g vermicelli rice noodles
100 g smoked salmon
1 tsp extra virgin olive oil
1 tbsp capers
2 medium mushrooms, diced
1/2 C. cabbage, diced

1 tbsp soy sauce
1 tbsp sweet chili sauce
1/4 tsp ground black pepper

## Directions

1. Prepare the noodles by following the instructions on the package. Drain it.
2. Get a large mixing bowl: Mix in it the noodles with the rest of the ingredients except for the rice paper sheets.
3. Place the filling in the fridge for 12 min.
4. Place a rice sheet in some warm water for 2 min. Drain it and place it on a kitchen towel.
5. Spoon 1/4 of the filling on one side of it. Pull the sides of the sheet over the filling then roll it tightly.
6. Repeat the process with the remaining ingredients.
7. Serve your wraps immediately with your favorite dipping sauce.
8. Enjoy.

# SKINNY
# Hot Fish Tacos

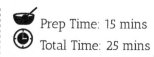

Prep Time: 15 mins
Total Time: 25 mins

Servings per Recipe: 4
| | |
|---|---|
| Calories | 259.6 |
| Fat | 12.4g |
| Cholesterol | 52.1mg |
| Sodium | 561.7mg |
| Carbohydrates | 13.5g |
| Protein | 25.5g |

## Ingredients

1 lb salmon, cubed
1 tbsp cumin
1 tsp chili powder
2 tbsp olive oil
1 medium yellow onion, chopped
2 limes, quartered
2 cans diced tomatoes with green

chilies, drained
1/2 bunch fresh cilantro, chopped
1 bunch green onion, chopped

## Directions

1. Get a mixing bowl: Stir in it the salmon with cumin, chili powder, a pinch of salt and pepper.
2. Place a large pan over medium heat. Heat the oil in it. Add the onion and cook it for 3 min.
3. Stir in the salmon then cook them over high heat for 3 to 4 min.
4. Place the salmon in the tortillas then top them with salsa, sour cream, sliced avocado, and crisp romaine lettuce.
5. Serve your tacos right away.
6. Enjoy.

# Alaskan
# Empanadas

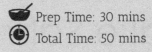 Prep Time: 30 mins

Total Time: 50 mins

Servings per Recipe: 16
| | |
|---|---|
| Calories | 165.2 |
| Fat | 10.7g |
| Cholesterol | 5.7mg |
| Sodium | 264.1mg |
| Carbohydrates | 13.5g |
| Protein | 3.4g |

## Ingredients

Empanadas
1 (15 oz.) boxes Pillsbury refrigerated pie
crusts
6 oz. smoked salmon, flaked
1 (5 1/4 oz.) packages boursin spreadable
cheese with garlic and herbs
Dip

1/2 C. sour cream
1 tbsp. chopped chives, if desired
paprika, for sprinkling

## Directions

1. Set your oven to 425 degrees F before doing anything else and line a baking sheet with the parchment paper.
2. Arrange the pie crusts onto a smooth surface.
3. Cut each crust into 4 wedges.
4. In a bowl, add the cheese and salmon and mix well.
5. Place about 2 tbsp. of the salmon mixture onto half of each crust wedge, leaving 1/4-inch border.
6. With wet fingers, moisten the edges of each wedge.
7. Fold the dough over the filling to form the triangles and press the edges to seal.
8. In the bottom of the prepared baking sheet, arrange the empanadas.
9. Cook in the oven for about 12-17 minutes.
10. Enjoy warm.
11. Remove from the oven and place the baking sheets onto a wire rack for about 10 minutes.
12. For the dip: in a bowl, add the sour cream, chives and paprika and gently, stir to combine.
13. Cut each empanada in half and enjoy alongside the dip.

# SARANAC
# Lake Salmon

Prep Time: 10 mins
Total Time: 15 mins

Servings per Recipe: 4
| | |
|---|---|
| Calories | 513.3 |
| Fat | 35.1 g |
| Cholesterol | 135.1 mg |
| Sodium | 272.3 mg |
| Carbohydrates | 0.7 g |
| Protein | 46.8 g |

## Ingredients

2 lbs. salmon fillets, cut into 4 pieces
1/4 C. vegetable oil
3 tbsp dill, chopped
salt & ground black pepper
4 tbsp melted butter

1/2 lemon, sliced
parsley

## Directions

1. Get a mixing bowl: Combine in it the oil with dill, salt, and pepper.
2. Coat the salmon pieces with the mixture. Let them sit for 25 min in the fridge.
3. Before you do anything, preheat the grill and grease it.
4. Drain the salmon pieces and grill them for 4 to 5 min on each side. Serve them warm.
5. Enjoy.

# 5-Ingredient
# Salmon

Prep Time: 5 mins
Total Time: 15 mins

Servings per Recipe: 4
| | |
|---|---|
| Calories | 414.4 |
| Fat | 29.5 g |
| Cholesterol | 93.5 mg |
| Sodium | 391.2 mg |
| Carbohydrates | 0.1 g |
| Protein | 34.8 g |

## Ingredients

1/3 C. basil, chopped
2 tbsp olive oil
1/2 tsp salt

1/4 tsp ground pepper
4 (6 oz.) salmon steaks

## Directions

1. Before you do anything, preheat the grill and grease it.
2. Get a mixing bowl: Mix in it the basil, olive oil, salt, and pepper.
3. Add the salmon pieces and toss them to coat.
4. Place them on the grill and cook them for 5 to 6 min on each side. Serve them warm.
5. Enjoy.

# NEW ENGLAND
# Egg Salad

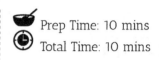 Prep Time: 10 mins

Total Time: 10 mins

Servings per Recipe: 6

| | |
|---|---|
| Calories | 178.2 |
| Fat | 8.6g |
| Cholesterol | 240.7mg |
| Sodium | 341.3mg |
| Carbohydrates | 2.9g |
| Protein | 21.9g |

## Ingredients

14 -15 ounces canned salmon, flaked
6 hard-boiled eggs, peeled and chopped
1/2 C. chopped onion
1/2 cucumber, peeled, seeded and chopped
1 1/2 tsps. Dijon mustard
1/2-3/4 C. mayonnaise

1/8 tsp. black pepper
1/2-3/4 tsp. dried tarragon
1/4 tsp. paprika
salt

## Directions

1. Place salmon, eggs, onion, cucumber, mustard, mayonnaise, pepper, tarragon and paprika in a bowl and combine well.
2. Add salt .
3. Leave in the refrigerator to chill prior to serving.
4. Enjoy.

# *Sweet and Sour*
# Grilled Fish

🥣 Prep Time: 5 mins
🕐 Total Time: 15 mins

Servings per Recipe: 2
Calories            418.0
Fat                 23.2 g
Cholesterol         93.5 mg
Sodium              230.7 mg
Carbohydrates       15.4 g
Protein             35.3 g

## Ingredients

1 1/2 tbsp honey
1 1/2 tbsp Dijon mustard
1 tbsp balsamic vinegar
1/4 tsp ground pepper

1/4 tsp garlic salt
2 (6 oz.) salmon steaks
cooking spray

## Directions

1. Set your grill for medium-high heat and grease the grill grate.
2. In a bowl, add all the ingredients except the salmon steaks and mix until well combined.
3. Add the salmon steaks and coat with the mixture generously.
4. Place the salmon steaks onto the grill and cook, covered for about 4-6 minutes, flipping once half way through.
5. Enjoy hot.

# CRUSTED
# Grilled Salmon

Prep Time: 20 mins
Total Time: 40 mins

Servings per Recipe: 8
| | |
|---|---|
| Calories | 264.4 |
| Fat | 10.9 g |
| Cholesterol | 77.4 mg |
| Sodium | 129.6 mg |
| Carbohydrates | 5.3 g |
| Protein | 35.3 g |

## Ingredients

8 (6 oz.) salmon fillets, skinless
2 cedar planks, soaked in water for 4 to
6 hours
1 tbsp dry barbecue spice
sea salt
1 large lemon
Crust
1 C. fresh dill, chopped
1/2 C. shallot, chopped

2 garlic cloves, chopped
2 green onions, chopped
3 tbsp cracked black pepper
2 tbsp olive oil
1 lemon, juice

## Directions

1. Set your grill for high heat and grease the grill grate.
2. Season the salmon fillets with the BBQ seasoning evenly.
3. For the crust: in a bowl, add all the ingredients and mix well.
4. Coat the flesh side of the salmon fillets with the crust mixture generously.
5. Sprinkle the soaked cedar planks with the salt, and place onto the grill.
6. Close lid of the grill and heat for about 3-5 minutes.
7. Arrange the salmon fillets on hot planks, skinned side down and cook, covered for about 12-15 minutes.
8. Enjoy with a drizzling of the lemon juice.

# Glazed
# Dijon Salmon

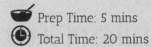 Prep Time: 5 mins
Total Time: 20 mins

Servings per Recipe: 4
Calories                435.6
Fat                     15.0 g
Cholesterol             78.4 mg
Sodium                  3589.9 mg
Carbohydrates           32.2 g
Protein                 46.1 g

## Ingredients

1/3 C. orange juice
1/3 C. soy sauce
1/4 C. honey
1 tbsp Dijon mustard
1 inch ginger, chopped
2 garlic cloves, minced

3 green onions, chopped
1 1/2 lb. salmon fillets

## Directions

1. In a bowl, add all the ingredients except the salmon fillets and mix until well combined.
2. Add the salmon fillets and coat with the marinade generously.
3. Place in the fridge for about 20-25 minutes.
4. Set your grill for medium-high heat and grease the grill grate.
5. Cook the salmon fillets onto the grill for about 10-12 minutes, flipping once half way through.
6. Enjoy hot.

# CLASSIC
# Grilled Teriyaki Salmon

 Prep Time: 8 hrs

Total Time: 8 hrs 12 min

Servings per Recipe: 4
| | |
|---|---|
| Calories | 272.8 |
| Fat | 5.0g |
| Cholesterol | 52.3mg |
| Sodium | 2845.8m |
| Carbohydrates | 28.6g |
| Protein | 27.6g |

## Ingredients

1 lb salmon fillet
1 C. teriyaki sauce or 1 C. teriyaki marinade

1/4 C. honey

## Directions

1.  Get a large bag: Place it in the salmon fillets with teriyaki sauce. Seal the bag and shake it to coat.
2.  Before you do anything preheat the grill and grease it.
3.  Remove the salmon fillets from the marinade. Cook it on the grill with skin side facing up for 4 min.
4.  Rotate the fillet on the other side and cook it for another 4 min. Flip the salmon fillet and brush it with honey. Cook it for 7 min then serve it warm.
5.  Enjoy

# New Jersey
# Diner Inspired Chowder

Prep Time: 35 mins
Total Time: 1 hr 40 mins

Servings per Recipe: 8
| | |
|---|---|
| Calories | 205 kcal |
| Fat | 9.5 g |
| Carbohydrates | 20.5g |
| Protein | 8.5 g |
| Cholesterol | 25 mg |
| Sodium | 561 mg |

## Ingredients

2 tbsp butter
1 tbsp olive oil
1 C. chopped onion
2 cloves garlic, chopped
1/2 C. chopped celery
1/2 C. all-purpose flour
6 C. chicken broth
1 lb. potatoes - peeled and cubed
1 tsp dried dill weed
1 tsp dried tarragon
1 tsp dried thyme

1/2 tsp paprika
8 oz. smoked salmon, cut into 1/2 inch pieces
1/4 C. white wine
1 tbsp fresh lemon juice
1/4 tsp hot sauce
1 tsp salt
1 tsp fresh-ground black pepper
1 C. half and half

## Directions

1. In a large span, mix together the butter, olive oil, onion, garlic and celery on medium-high heat and cook for 8-10 minutes.
2. Add the flour and stir to combine well.
3. Slowly, add the chicken broth and stir till mixture becomes slightly thick.
4. Stir in the potatoes, dill, tarragon, thyme and paprika.
5. Reduce the heat to medium and simmer, covered for about 15 minutes.
6. Stir in the salmon, wine, lemon juice, hot sauce, salt and pepper.
7. Reduce the heat to low and simmer, uncovered for about 10 minutes.
8. Stir in the half-and-half and simmer for about 30 minutes, stirring occasionally.
9. Serve hot.

# SOUR
# Salmon

Prep Time: 20 mins
Total Time: 50 mins

Servings per Recipe: 4
| | |
|---|---|
| Calories | 607 kcal |
| Fat | 42.5 g |
| Carbohydrates | 5.7g |
| Protein | 49.8 g |
| Cholesterol | 207 mg |
| Sodium | 965 mg |

## Ingredients

4 (6 oz.) thick salmon fillets
1 (6 oz.) can lump crabmeat, divided
4 slices smoked Gouda cheese
1/4 C. butter, melted
2 lemons, juiced - divided
1 (8 oz.) carton sour cream

1 tbsp finely chopped fresh dill
1 (2 oz.) jar capers in brine, drained

## Directions

1.  Set your oven to 350 degrees F before doing anything else.
2.  Trim the salmon fillets to remove thin portion.
3.  With a very sharp knife, cut the salmon fillets horizontally through the center but leave one end uncut so the fillet opens like a book.
4.  Place 1/4 of the lump crab meat over each opened fillet and top with a smoked Gouda slice.
5.  Close the fillets.
6.  In a small bowl, mix together the melted butter and juice of 1 lemon.
7.  Arrange each fillet into a single-serving baking dish and drizzle the lemon butter evenly.
8.  Cook in the oven for about 30 minutes.
9.  In a bowl, mix together the juice of the 2nd lemon, sour cream and dill.
10. Spread the sour cream mixture over each baked fillet evenly.
11. Serve immediately with a sprinkling of the capers.

# New England
# Salmon Chowder

Prep Time: 15 mins
Total Time: 45 mins

Servings per Recipe: 8

| | |
|---|---|
| Calories | 490 kcal |
| Fat | 25.9 g |
| Carbohydrates | 26.5g |
| Protein | 38.6 g |
| Cholesterol | 104 mg |
| Sodium | 1140 mg |

## Ingredients

3 tbsp butter
3/4 C. chopped onion
1/2 C. chopped celery
1 tsp garlic powder
2 C. diced potatoes
2 carrots, diced
2 C. chicken broth
1 tsp salt
1 tsp ground black pepper

1 tsp dried dill weed
2 (16 oz.) cans salmon
1 (12 fluid oz.) can evaporated milk
1 (15 oz.) can creamed corn
1/2 lb. Cheddar cheese, shredded

## Directions

1. In a large pan, melt the butter on medium heat and sauté the onion, celery and garlic powder till tender.
2. Stir in the potatoes, carrots, broth, salt, pepper and dill and bring to a boil.
3. Reduce the heat and simmer, covered for about 20 minutes.
4. Stir in the salmon, evaporated milk, corn and cheese and cook till heated completely.

# SPANISH
# American Inspired Ceviche

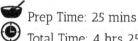 Prep Time: 25 mins
Total Time: 4 hrs 25 mii

Servings per Recipe: 6
| | |
|---|---|
| Calories | 288 kca |
| Fat | 22.6 g |
| Carbohydrates | 5.9 g |
| Protein | 16.1 g |
| Cholesterol | 45 mg |
| Sodium | 2253 mg |

## Ingredients

1/4 tsp white sugar
2 1/2 tbsp sea salt
1/2 tsp chili paste
1/4 C. fresh lime juice
1/4 tsp fresh ground pepper
1/4 tsp cumin
1/4 C. extra virgin olive oil
1 clove garlic, minced
1/4 C. minced red onion

1 ripe tomato, finely diced
2 tbsp minced fresh cilantro
1 lb. very fresh salmon fillets, thinly slicec
1 avocado, sliced

## Directions

1. In a large glass bowl, add the sugar, salt, chili paste and lime juice and till sugar dissolves.
2. Stir in the olive oil, garlic, onion, tomato, cilantro, pepper and cumin.
3. Gently stir in the salmon.
4. Refrigerate, covered for about 4 hours.
5. Before serving, drain the excess liquid from the salmon.
6. Gently stir in the avocado slices and keep aside for about 15 minutes.

# Brown Sugar
# Ginger Salmon

Prep Time: 5 mins
Total Time: 25 mins

Servings per Recipe: 4
| | |
|---|---|
| Calories | 377 kcal |
| Fat | 13.7 g |
| Carbohydrates | 13.4g |
| Protein | 48.4 g |
| Cholesterol | 100 mg |
| Sodium | 519 mg |

## Ingredients

4 (8 oz.) fresh salmon fillets
salt to taste
1/3 C. cold water
1/4 C. seasoned rice vinegar
2 tbsps brown sugar
1 tbsp hot chili paste
1 tbsp finely grated fresh ginger

4 cloves garlic, diced
1 tsp soy sauce
1/4 C. diced fresh basil

## Directions

1.  Heat up your grill or grilling plate. Then oil it.
2.  Coat your salmon piece with some salt.
3.  Cook it on the grill for about 8 to 10 mins per side.
4.  Once the salmon is ready it should flake when broken with a fork.
5.  Get a saucepan, or small pot, and combine: soy sauce, water, garlic, rice vinegar, chili paste, and brown sugar.
6.  Get the contents boiling then set the heat to low and let it simmer for 4 mins until thick.
7.  Cover your salmon with this mix and also some basil.
8.  Enjoy.

# KERALA
# Salmon

Prep Time: 20 mins
Total Time: 30 mins

Servings per Recipe: 2
| | |
|---|---|
| Calories | 765 kcal |
| Fat | 47.1 g |
| Carbohydrates | 11g |
| Protein | 81.5 g |
| Cholesterol | 1262 mg |
| Sodium | 1783 mg |

## Ingredients

2 tbsp olive oil
3/4 tsp cumin seeds
1/2 tsp brown mustard seeds
1 small onion, sliced into thin half-circles
1 clove garlic, minced
1 tbsp minced fresh ginger root
1 green chili pepper, chopped
10 fresh curry leaves, chopped
(optional)

1 tomato, diced
2 (14.75 oz.) cans salmon, drained and bones removed
1/4 C. chopped fresh cilantro

## Directions

1. In a skillet, heat the oil on medium heat and sauté the cumin and mustard seeds till the seeds begin to pop.
2. Stir in the onions and sauté till golden brown.
3. Stir in the garlic, ginger, chili pepper and curry leaves and sauté till the garlic becomes golden.
4. Add the tomatoes and sauté for a few seconds.
5. Stir in the salmon and with the back of the stirring spoon, break the salmon into small pieces.
6. Cook for about 5-10 minutes.
7. Remove from the heat and serve with a garnishing of the cilantro.

# *San Luis*
# Salmon

🥣 Prep Time: 20 mins
🕐 Total Time: 1 hr 30 mins

Servings per Recipe: 4

| | |
|---|---|
| Calories | 394 kcal |
| Fat | 21.6 g |
| Carbohydrates | 11.9g |
| Protein | 38.2 g |
| Cholesterol | 119 mg |
| Sodium | 298 mg |

## Ingredients

2 tbsp olive oil
2 limes, juiced
2 marinated roasted red peppers, with liquid
1 clove garlic, finely chopped
1/8 tsp ground allspice
1/8 tsp ground cinnamon
1/4 tsp ground cumin
1/4 tsp white sugar

salt and pepper to taste
1 1/2 lb. salmon steaks
1 large tomato, cut into thin wedges
3 green onions, chopped
1 C. shredded lettuce
1 lime, sliced

## Directions

1. In a large nonreactive bowl, mix together the olive oil, juice of the 2 limes, roasted red peppers, garlic, allspice, cinnamon, cumin, sugar, salt and pepper.
2. Add the salmon steaks and rub with the mixture evenly.
3. Refrigerate, covered for at least 1 hour.
4. Set the broiler of your oven.
5. In a broiler pan, place the salmon steaks in a single layer.
6. Cook under the broiler for about 3-5 minutes per side.
7. In a small bowl, mix together the tomato wedges and green onions.
8. Serve salmon with the tomato mixture, lettuce and lime wedges.

# SMOKED
# Feta Frittata

Prep Time: 15 mins
Total Time: 45 mins

Servings per Recipe: 6
Calories          303 kcal
Fat               17.8 g
Carbohydrates     16.1g
Protein           20.3 g
Cholesterol       399 mg
Sodium            530 mg

## Ingredients

2 tbsp butter
2 C. chopped kale, or to taste
2 tbsp water
2 potatoes, cut into 1/4-inch slices
4 oz smoked salmon, finely chopped

1 tbsp capers
12 eggs, beaten
3 oz crumbled feta cheese

## Directions

1.  Preheat the oven broiler. Place the rack 6 inches away from the heat.
2.  Place a large oven proof pan over medium heat. Cook in it the butter until it melts. Add the kale and cook it for 3 min.
3.  Stir in the water and put on the lid. Place the lid aside and keep cooking the kale while stirring until no water is left.
4.  Stir in the potatoes, salmon, and capers. Cook them for 4 min. Spread the mix in the pan and pour the eggs all over it to cover it.
5.  Cook the mix for 6 min while stirring gently then spread it again to cover the bottom of the pan. Top it with cheese.
6.  Cook it in the oven for 6 min. Serve your Frittata warm.
7.  Enjoy.

# *Creamy* Olives and Salmon Frittata

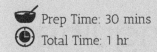

🥣 Prep Time: 30 mins
🕐 Total Time: 1 hr

Servings per Recipe: 4
| | |
|---|---|
| Calories | 401 kcal |
| Fat | 35.9 g |
| Carbohydrates | 3.2g |
| Protein | 17.3 g |
| Cholesterol | 327 mg |
| Sodium | 504 mg |

## Ingredients

4 tbsp olive oil
1/4 medium onion, chopped
salt and pepper to taste
4 oz pepper smoked salmon
8 black olives, chopped

6 eggs
2 tbsp milk
2 tbsp heavy cream
1/2 (8 oz) package cream cheese, cubed

## Directions

1. Before you do anything preheat the oven to 350 F. Coat a casserole dish with some butter or oil.
2. Place a large oven proof pan over medium heat. Heat the oil in it. Add the onion with a pinch of salt and pepper. Cook them for 3 min.
3. Stir in the olives with salmon. Cook them while stirring all the time for 2 min.
4. Get a mixing bowl: Combine in it the eggs, milk and cream. Mix them well. Spread it over the cooked salmon and onion mix.
5. Lay the cream cheese dices on top. Cook the Frittata until it is cooked in the bottom. Transfer the pan to the oven. Cook it for 22 min.
6. Serve your Frittata warm.
7. Enjoy.

# RESTAURANT STYLE
# Linguine

Prep Time: 10 mins

Total Time: 20 mins

Servings per Recipe: 4

| | |
|---|---|
| Calories | 583 kcal |
| Carbohydrates | 64.4 g |
| Cholesterol | 205 mg |
| Fat | 27.1 g |
| Protein | 21 g |
| Sodium | 373 mg |

## Ingredients

2 (8 oz) packages fresh linguine pasta
1 C. cream
4 oz smoked salmon, chopped
1 pinch freshly grated nutmeg (optional)
1 1/2 tbsps black caviar

1 pinch ground black pepper, or to taste
(optional)
1 bunch chopped flat leaf parsley

## Directions

1. Boil your pasta in water and salt for 7 to 10 mins until al dente. Drain the liquid and set aside.

2. Get a saucepan and heat up your cream, then cook your salmon with pepper and nutmeg. Coat the pasta with this mixture. Add caviar as well.

3. Garnish everything with some parsley.

4. Enjoy.

# *Chipotle* Salmon

🍲 Prep Time: 15 mins
🕐 Total Time: 23 mins

Servings per Recipe: 4
| | |
|---|---|
| Calories | 331.3 |
| Fat | 15.6g |
| Cholesterol | 77.4mg |
| Sodium | 618.3mg |
| Carbohydrates | 12.2g |
| Protein | 36.4g |

## Ingredients

4 medium tomatillos, husked and rinsed
1/4 C. green onion, chopped
1/4 C. fresh cilantro, chopped
1 1/2 tbsp fresh lime juice
1 ripe avocado, seeded and diced
1 tsp jalapeno, seeded and minced
1 1/2 tbsp chili powder

1/2 tsp cumin
1 tbsp brown sugar
1 tsp kosher salt
4 (6 oz.) wild copper river salmon fillets

## Directions

1. In a pan, add the tomatillo and enough water to cover and bring to a boil.
2. Simmer for about 5 minutes.
3. Remove the tomatillos and keep aside to cool. When cool, then chop them roughly.
4. In a large bowl, mix together the tomatillos, onion, cilantro, lime juice and salt.
5. Gently fold in the avocado and jalapeño.
6. Set your oven to 350 degrees.
7. In a bowl, mix together the chili powder, cumin, sugar and salt.
8. Coat the fish with the spice mix.
9. Heat a large oven-proof nonstick skillet on medium heat and cook the salmon rub side down for about 2 minutes.
10. Flip the fish and transfer the skillet into the oven and cook for about 5-6 minutes.
11. Transfer the fish fillets into the serving plates and serve with a topping of the salsa.

# ORANGE
# Serrano Salmon on Grill

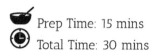

Prep Time: 15 mins
Total Time: 30 mins

Servings per Recipe: 6
| | |
|---|---|
| Calories | 293.3 |
| Fat | 11.4g |
| Cholesterol | 98.5mg |
| Sodium | 129.3mg |
| Carbohydrates | 10.1g |
| Protein | 38.7g |

## Ingredients

SALSA
1 navel orange, peeled, segmented
2 lemons, peeled, segmented
2 tsp seeded serrano chilies, minced
3/4 C. canned tomatillo, diced
1/2 C. red onion, diced
1/4 C. cilantro, chopped
1/2 tsp sugar
1 tsp fresh oregano
salt and pepper

SALMON
2 1/2 lb. fresh salmon fillets, skinless
2 tbsp vegetable oil
2 tbsp lemon juice
salt and pepper

## Directions

1. Set your grill for medium-high heat and lightly, grease the grill grate.
2. Chop the orange and lemon segments roughly, retaining all the accumulate juice.
3. In a bowl, add the citrus fruit, juice and remaining salsa Ingredients and toss to coat well.
4. Refrigerate till before serving.
5. For salmon in a large bowl, add the oil, lemon juice, salt and pepper and mix till well combined.
6. Coat the salmon with the oil mixture generously.
7. Cook the salmon fillets on the grill for about 8 minutes, flipping once.
8. Serve the salmon with a topping of the salsa.

# *Salmon*
# Appetizer Bowl

🥣 Prep Time: 5 mins
🕐 Total Time: 1 hr

Servings per Recipe: 2
| | |
|---|---|
| Calories | 204.6 |
| Fat | 13.9 g |
| Cholesterol | 29.1mg |
| Sodium | 48.2mg |
| Carbohydrates | 9.1g |
| Protein | 12.9 g |

## Ingredients

4 oz. salmon fillets, 3/4 to 1-inch thick
1/2 medium avocado
1/4 small cucumber, halved, seeded and cut into spears
1/2 C. grape tomatoes, halved
1/2 C. escarole
2 tbsp lemon juice, fresh only

2 tsp olive oil
fresh ground pepper
nonstick cooking spray

## Directions

1. Set your oven to 425 degrees F before doing anything else and lightly, grease a shallow baking dish with the cooking spray.
2. Season the salmon fillets with the salt and pepper and arrange into the prepared baking dish.
3. Cook in the oven for about 10-12 minutes.
4. Remove from the oven and keep aside to cool for about 10 minutes.
5. Remove the skin of salmon fillets and discard.
6. Break the salmon fillets into large chunks.
7. Transfer the salmon chunks into a plate and refrigerate to chill for about 30 minutes.
8. In a small bowl, mix together the lemon juice and olive oil.
9. In martini glasses, place the salmon chunks, avocado, cucumber, tomatoes, and escarole.
10. Drizzle with the oil mixture and sprinkle with the pepper.
11. Refrigerate, covered to chill before serving.

# HANDMADE
# Full Party Platter

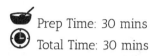

Prep Time: 30 mins
Total Time: 30 mins

| Servings per Recipe: 12 | |
| --- | --- |
| Calories | 612.0 |
| Fat | 40.7g |
| Cholesterol | 46.2mg |
| Sodium | 1309.8mg |
| Carbohydrates | 45.5g |
| Protein | 24.7g |

## Ingredients

12 spinach tortillas
1 C. raisins
1 C. dried cranberries
1 C. olive
1 C. cream cheese
1 C. pomegranate
1 C. nuts
1 C. peanut butter
1 C. white radish
1 C. shredded cooked chicken
1 C. sliced beet
1 C. red cabbage
1 C. smoked salmon
1 C. shredded carrot
1 C. diced ham, optional
1 C. bacon bits, optional
1 C. pineapple
1 C. arugula
1 C. red leaf lettuce
1 C. butter lettuce

1 C. endive
1 8 oz. cans green olives
1 C. escarole
1 C. smoked turkey
1 C. watercress
1 C. cucumber
1 C. mayonnaise
1 C. fresh basil
1 C. lemon zest
1 C. fresh dill
1 C. Brussels sprout
1 C. lima beans
1 C. green onion
1 C. honey mustard
1 C. toasted almond
1 C. canned peaches

## Directions

1. For first cream cheese spread, mix the softened cream cheese with any of these ingredients like the basil, dried cranberries, lemon zest, olives and pomegranate.
2. For the honey grilled chicken, prepared a spread with the mixing of the nuts, raisins, a dollop of peanut butter and use with the butter lettuce.
3. For a spinach wrap, mix together the smoked salmon, cucumbers, white radishes, green

olives and escarole.

4. For the red leaf lettuce wrap, mix together the fresh beets, cranberries, cream cheese and smoked turkey.

5. For a second cream cheese spread, mix the cream cheese with the roasted honey, nuts, raisin, cream cheese, shredded carrot, ham chunks and watercress.

6. For the mustard spread, mix together the Brussels sprouts, lima beans, bacon, honey mustard, cranberries, green onions and Arugula.

7. For the third cream cheese spread, mix together the cream cheese with the smoked turkey, chunks of pineapple, peaches and Endive.

# MARIA'S
# Potluck Chowder

Prep Time: 20 mins
Total Time: 1 hr 20 min

Servings per Recipe: 6

| | |
|---|---|
| Calories | 1144 kca |
| Fat | 63.3 g |
| Carbohydrates | 93.1g |
| Protein | 48.4 g |
| Cholesterol | 155 mg |
| Sodium | 2405 mg |

## Ingredients

10 slices turkey bacon, chopped
2 large onions, finely chopped
4 stalks celery, finely chopped
3 carrots, finely chopped
5 green onions, finely chopped
1/3 C. chopped fresh parsley
1/2 C. water
6 C. fish stock
Salt to taste
1 1/2 tbsp ground black pepper
1 1/2 tbsp dried dill weed

8 red potatoes, cubed
1 C. butter
1 C. all-purpose flour
5 C. milk
3/4 C. white wine
1/4 C. lemon juice
1 1/2 lb. flaked or chopped smoked salmon
1 1/2 C. frozen corn kernels

## Directions

1. Heat a large pan on medium heat and cook the bacon for a few minutes to release some of the drippings.
2. Add the onions and celery and sauté till tender.
3. Stir in the carrots, green onions, parsley, water, fish stock, salt, pepper and dill.
4. Reduce the heat to low and simmer, covered for about 15 minutes.
5. Stir in the potatoes and simmer for about 20 minutes.
6. Meanwhile in a small skillet, melt the butter on medium heat.
7. Stir in the flour and cook till smooth and light brown, stirring continuously.
8. Slowly, add the milk, a little bit at a time of the milk, beating continuously.
9. Add the roux and remaining milk into the pan with the vegetables and cook till heated completely, stirring continuously.
10. Stir in the white wine, lemon juice, smoked salmon and corn and cook till heated completely. Serve immediately

# 2-Cheese Red Potato Chowder

Prep Time: 15 mins
Total Time: 1 hr 5 mins

Servings per Recipe: 6
| | |
|---|---|
| Calories | 388 kcal |
| Fat | 13.1 g |
| Carbohydrates | 46.5g |
| Protein | 22.8 g |
| Cholesterol | 37 mg |
| Sodium | 417 mg |

## Ingredients

5 small red potatoes cut into bite-size pieces
2 tbsp olive oil
1 onion, diced
2 stalks celery, thinly sliced
2 tbsp all-purpose flour
1/2 tsp salt
1/4 tsp ground black pepper
4 C. 2% milk

1 cooked salmon fillet, flaked
1 1/4 C. frozen peas
1 1/4 C. frozen corn
1 tsp dried dill weed
1/2 C. shredded reduced-fat Swiss cheese
1/2 C. shredded reduced-fat Cheddar cheese
1 green onion, finely chopped

## Directions

1. In a large pan of salted water, add the potatoes and bring to a boil.
2. Reduce the heat to medium-low and simmer for about 20 minutes.
3. Drain the potatoes well.
4. In a large pan, heat the olive oil on medium-high heat and sauté the onion and celery for about 5-7 minutes.
5. Add the flour, salt and pepper and stir till well combined.
6. Slowly, add the milk and bring to a boil, stirring continuously.
7. Reduce the heat to medium and simmer for about 10 minutes.
8. Add the potatoes, flaked salmon, peas, corn, and dill and cook for about 10 minutes.
9. Stir in the Swiss cheese and Cheddar cheese and cook for about 5 minutes.
10. Serve hot with a garnishing of the green onion.

# LEMON
# Pepper Seafood Sampler Chowder

 Prep Time: 20 mins
Total Time: 1 hr

Servings per Recipe: 8
Calories          434 kcal
Fat               24.4 g
Carbohydrates     30.8g
Protein           23.9 g
Cholesterol       144 mg
Sodium            1499 mg

## Ingredients

1/4 C. butter
3 tbsp minced garlic
1/3 C. flour
4 C. half-and-half
1 C. dry vegetable soup mix
1/2 C. dried onion flakes
2 tbsp lemon pepper
1 pinch dried thyme
1 pinch saffron

1 C. diced salmon
1 C. diced halibut
1 C. peeled and deveined shrimp
1 C. peeled and deveined prawns
1 C. scallops

## Directions

1. In a large pan, add the butter and garlic on medium-high heat and cook till the butter is melted.
2. Stir in the flour and cook for about 1 minute, beating continuously.
3. Slowly, add the half-and-half and cook till smooth, beating continuously.
4. Add the vegetable soup mix, onion flakes, lemon pepper, thyme and saffron and cook for about 5-10 minutes, stirring occasionally.
5. Stir in the salmon, halibut, shrimp, prawns and scallops and bring to a simmer.
6. Reduce the heat to medium-low and simmer for about 30 minutes, stirring occasionally.

# *Grandma's*
# Salmon Croquettes

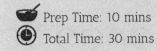

Prep Time: 10 mins
Total Time: 30 mins

Servings per Recipe: 6
| | |
|---|---|
| Calories | 277.8 |
| Fat | 11.1g |
| Cholesterol | 123.7mg |
| Sodium | 477.2mg |
| Carbohydrates | 22.5g |
| Protein | 20.8g |

## Ingredients

1 (14 oz.) cans salmon, drained
1 medium onion ( grated )
salt and pepper
1/4 C. flour
1 1/2 C. milk
1/4 tsp garlic powder
1 C. seasoned bread crumbs

2 eggs, beaten
2 tbsp butter
sunflower oil ( for frying)

## Directions

1. In a large frying pan, melt the butter on medium-high heat and sauté the onion and garlic powder till tender.
2. Add the salmon, salt and pepper and cook till heated completely.
3. Add the flour and stir till well combined.
4. Slowly, add the milk, stirring continuously till the mixture becomes thick and forms a ball.
5. Transfer the mixture into a plate and keep aside to cool completely.
6. Make oval shaped croquettes from the mixture.
7. Dip the croquettes in beaten eggs and then coat with the bread crumbs.
8. In a deep skillet, heat the oil and deep fry till golden brown from both sides.
9. Transfer the croquettes onto a paper towel lined plate to drain.

# ASIAN
# Mango Salmon Curry

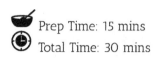

Prep Time: 15 mins
Total Time: 30 mins

Servings per Recipe: 4
| | |
|---|---|
| Calories | 330 kcal |
| Fat | 20.6 g |
| Carbohydrates | 12.2g |
| Protein | 25 g |
| Cholesterol | 50 mg |
| Sodium | 91 mg |

## Ingredients

1 (1 lb.) salmon fillet
1/4 C. avocado oil
1 tsp curry powder
salt to taste
1 mango - peeled, seeded, and diced

1/4 C. diced red onion
1 small serrano pepper, diced
1 small bunch cilantro leaves
1 lime

## Directions

1. Set your oven to 400 degrees F before doing anything else and line a baking sheet with a piece of the foil.
2. Arrange the salmon fillet onto the prepared baking sheet and fold the edges of foil over the salmon and crimp to seal.
3. Cook in the oven for about 15 minutes.
4. In a small bowl, mix together the avocado oil, curry powder and salt.
5. Transfer the salmon onto a serving platter and drizzle with the avocado oil mixture.
6. Top with the mango, red onion and Serrano pepper.
7. Drizzle with lime juice and serve with a garnishing of the cilantro.

# Summer
# Fruit Curry Dinner

🥣 Prep Time: 30 mins
🕐 Total Time: 1 hr

Servings per Recipe: 4
| | |
|---|---|
| Calories | 592.9 |
| Fat | 25.9 g |
| Cholesterol | 260.1 mg |
| Sodium | 1506.1 mg |
| Carbohydrates | 33.8 g |
| Protein | 59.1 g |

## Ingredients

1 (14 oz.) can coconut milk
1 - 2 tbsp yellow Thai curry paste, see appendix
1 1/2 C. fish stock
3 tbsp fish sauce (recommended ( Nam Pla)
2 tbsp sugar
3 stalks lemongrass, each cut into 1/3 's and bruised with the flat of a knife
3 fresh lime leaves, stalked and cut into strips (optional)

1/2 tsp turmeric
2 1/4 lb. pumpkin, peeled and cut into large, bite-sized chunks
18 oz. salmon fillets, preferably organic, skinned and cut into large, bite-sized chunks
18 oz. peeled raw shrimp
bok choy
1/2-1 lime, juice of
cilantro, for garnish

## Directions

1. Scoop the thick creamy top from the can of coconut milk and transfer into a large pan on medium heat.
2. Add the curry paste and with a wooden spoon, beat till well combined.
3. Slowly, add the remaining coconut milk, beating continuously.
4. Add the fish stock, fish sauce, sugar, lemon grass, lime leaves and turmeric and bring to a boil.
5. Add the pumpkin and cook for about 15 minutes.
6. Add the salmon and shrimp and cook for about 3-4 minutes.
7. Stir in the bok choy and cook till wilted.
8. Stir in the juice of half a lime and remove from the heat.
9. Serve the curry with a garnishing of the cilantro.

# HONEY
# Garlic Salmon

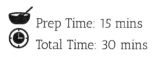 Prep Time: 15 mins
Total Time: 30 mins

| Servings per Recipe: 4 | |
| --- | --- |
| Calories | 481 kcal |
| Fat | 31.1 g |
| Carbohydrates | 17.5g |
| Protein | 35.2 g |
| Cholesterol | 114 mg |
| Sodium | 2071 mg |

## Ingredients

1 bunch fresh mint, stems removed
1 bunch flat-leaf parsley, stems
removed
1/2 C. fresh lemon juice
4 cloves garlic, peeled
2 tbsps honey
2 tbsps olive oil
4 tsps kosher salt
1 tsp freshly ground black pepper

4 (6 oz.) salmon fillets
2 tbsps butter, melted
1 lemon, thinly sliced
4 small mint sprigs for garnish

## Directions

1. Begin to pulse the following in a blender: pepper, parsley, salt, mint, olive oil, honey, garlic, and lemon juice.

2. Work the mix until it is smooth then marinate your fish with the mix for about 10 mins.

3. Get an outdoor grill hot and coat the grate with oil. Then cook your fish on the grill for about 3 mins per side. Top your fish with some butter and serve with some lemon pieces and mint sprigs.

4. Enjoy.

# *Alaskan*
# Citrus Salmon

🥣 Prep Time: 15 mins
🕐 Total Time: 40 mins

Servings per Recipe: 2
| | |
|---|---|
| Calories | 598 kcal |
| Fat | 25.1 g |
| Carbohydrates | 23.2g |
| Protein | 46.9 g |
| Cholesterol | 134 mg |
| Sodium | 139 mg |

## Ingredients

2 blood oranges, peeled and sliced into rounds
1 pound salmon fillets
1/2 tsp freshly grated nutmeg

1 C. red wine

## Directions

1. Set your oven to 350 degrees before doing anything else.
2. Place your oranges in a casserole dish. Then place the salmon over the oranges. Top everything with the nutmeg and then the wine.
3. Place a covering of foil on the dish and cook everything in the oven for 22 mins.
4. Enjoy.

# MONDAY'S
# Seafood Dinner

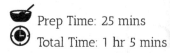

Prep Time: 25 mins
Total Time: 1 hr 5 mins

| Servings per Recipe: 4 | |
|---|---|
| Calories | 515 kcal |
| Fat | 24.4 g |
| Carbohydrates | 46.4g |
| Protein | 27.3 g |
| Cholesterol | 155 mg |
| Sodium | 701 mg |

## Ingredients

1 lb. small potatoes, scrubbed
1/2 (3 oz.) fillet skinless, boneless
halibut fillets
1/2 lb. skinless, boneless salmon fillets
2 C. milk
2 eggs, divided
2 tbsp butter

1 pinch ground nutmeg
1 dash Worcestershire sauce
salt and pepper to taste
1 C. dried bread crumbs, seasoned
1 C. oil for frying

## Directions

1. In a pan, add the potatoes and enough water to cover and bring to a boil.
2. Cook for about 15 minutes.
3. Meanwhile, in a large pan, place the halibut, salmon and milk and bring to a simmer.
4. Cook, covered for about 5 minutes.
5. Drain off the milk and keep the fish aside.
6. Drain the potatoes and place in a large bowl.
7. Add 1 egg and the butter and mash till smooth.
8. Stir in the nutmeg, Worcestershire sauce, salt and pepper.
9. Add the fish and gently mix, taking care not to break into too small of pieces.
10. In a shallow dish, beat the remaining egg.
11. In another shallow dish, place the bread crumbs.
12. With lightly floured hands, make the equal sized patties from the fish mixture.
13. Dip each patty into the egg, then coat with the breadcrumbs evenly.
14. Arrange the fish cakes onto a large plate and refrigerate for about 30 minutes.
15. In a large heavy skillet, heat 1/4 inch of the oil on medium to medium-high heat and fry the fish cakes for about 3 minutes per side. Serve fresh and hot.

# *Creamy*
# Curried Mushrooms with Salmon

🍲 Prep Time: 45 mins

🕐 Total Time: 1 hr 10 mins

Servings per Recipe: 4

| | |
|---|---|
| Calories | 599 kcal |
| Fat | 44.7 g |
| Carbohydrates | 16.5g |
| Protein | 34.3 g |
| Cholesterol | 182 mg |
| Sodium | 665 mg |

## Ingredients

4 (6 oz.) fillets fresh salmon
salt and black pepper to taste
1 tbsp butter
2 medium onions, diced
8 cloves garlic, minced
1 C. chopped Portobello mushrooms
1 C. fresh porcini mushrooms, cleaned and sliced
1/2 C. diced fennel bulb
1/2 C. diced celery

1 tsp curry powder
1/2 tsp saffron
2 C. chicken broth
1 C. heavy cream
1 tbsp butter
4 sprigs chopped fresh parsley for garnish
4 lemon slices for garnish
2 tbsps thinly sliced green onion for garnish

## Directions

1. Lay out your pieces of fish and top each one with pepper and salt.
2. Begin to stir fry your onions in 1 tbsp of butter for 6 mins then combine in the garlic and continue to stir fry everything for 60 more secs. Now add in your celery, fennel, and mushrooms.
3. Let everything fry for 6 mins. Add your pepper, curry powder, salt, and saffron. Stir everything and cook for 3 additional mins. Add in the chicken broth and heat the mix for 7 more mins while stirring. Add in heavy cream and stir again. Let the mix cook for about 6 more mins.
4. At the same time begin to fry your salmon pieces in 1 tbsp of butter with the skin on the pan. Increase the temperature of the stovetop burner and fry the fish for 2-3 mins for everything side.
5. Lay your plates for serving and place some mushroom mix on the plate then layer your fish over the mushroom then add some more sauce over the fish.
6. Enjoy.

# KALAMATA
# Fettuccini

Prep Time: 30 mins
Total Time: 1 hr

Servings per Recipe: 4
| | |
|---|---|
| Calories | 669 kcal |
| Fat | 28.7 g |
| Carbohydrates | 61.8g |
| Protein | 42.8 g |
| Cholesterol | 69 mg |
| Sodium | 989 mg |

## Ingredients

8 oz. dry fettuccini noodles
3 tbsp olive oil
1/2 C. finely chopped onion
1/2 C. finely chopped green bell pepper
2 tbsp dried Italian seasoning
1/2 C. pitted kalamata olives
1 lemon, juiced

1 (14.75 oz.) can red salmon, drained
1 (8 oz.) container light sour cream
1 (8 oz.) container low-fat plain yogurt
2 oz. blue cheese, crumbled

## Directions

1. In a large pan of lightly salted boiling water, cook the pasta for about 8-10 minutes.
2. Drain well and keep aside.
3. In a large skillet, heat the oil on medium heat and sauté the onion and bell pepper till soft and translucent.
4. Stir in the Italian seasoning, kalamata olives, lemon juice and cook for about 10 minutes.
5. Stir in the salmon, sour cream, yogurt and blue cheese and remove from the heat.
6. Add the cooked pasta and toss to coat well.

# Omega-3 Patties

Prep Time: 15 mins
Total Time: 1 hr

Servings per Recipe: 6

| | |
|---|---|
| Calories | 194 kcal |
| Fat | 9.3 g |
| Carbohydrates | 18.2g |
| Protein | 9.5 g |
| Cholesterol | 50 mg |
| Sodium | 354 mg |

## Ingredients

1/2 lb. salmon
1 red potato, peeled and chopped
1 shallot, minced
1 egg, beaten
1/4 C. Italian seasoned bread crumbs
1 tsp dried Italian seasoning
salt and pepper to taste

1/2 C. cornflake crumbs
2 tbsp olive oil

## Directions

1. Set your oven to 350 degrees F before doing anything else and lightly, grease a small baking dish.
2. Arrange the salmon into the prepared baking dish.
3. Cover the baking dish and cook in the oven for about 20 minutes.
4. In a small pan of the water, add the potatoes and bring to a boil.
5. Cook for about 15 minutes.
6. Drain the potatoes and then mash them.
7. In a bowl, add the salmon, potato, shallot, egg, bread crumbs, Italian seasoning, salt and pepper and mix till well combined.
8. In a shallow bowl, place the cornflake crumbs.
9. Make about 1-inch balls from the salmon mixture.
10. Coat the balls with the cornflakes crumb mixture evenly and then gently, press each ball into a patty.
11. In a medium pan, heat the olive oil on medium heat and fry the patties for about 3-5 minutes per side.

# SALMON
# Asian Style

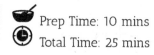
Prep Time: 10 mins
Total Time: 25 mins

Servings per Recipe: 4
Calories              36.5
Fat                   0.9g
Cholesterol           0.0mg
Sodium                42.8mg
Carbohydrates         25.3g
Protein               5.0g

## Ingredients

4 - 8 oz. salmon fillets
Asian plum sauce, to taste
1/2 C. green onion, chopped

## Directions

1. Set the broiler of your oven.
2. Coat the salmon fillets with the plum sauce evenly.
3. In a shallow baking dish, place the salmon fillets and top with half of the green onions.
4. Keep aside for about 10 minutes.
5. Cook under the broiler for about 10 - 20 minutes.
6. Check after 10 minutes.
7. Drizzle with the additional sauce and serve with a sprinkling of the remaining green onions.

# Orient Style
# Salmon

Prep Time: 15 mins
Total Time: 35 mins

Servings per Recipe: 24

| | |
|---|---|
| Calories | 473 kcal |
| Fat | 13.2 g |
| Carbohydrates | 55.9 g |
| Protein | 35.3 g |
| Cholesterol | 51 mg |
| Sodium | 540 mg |

## Ingredients

1/2 C. nonfat plain yogurt
3 scallions, sliced, whites and greens separated
2 tbsp lemon juice
2 tbsp chopped fresh cilantro
1/2 tsp ground cumin
3/4 tsp salt, divided
1/2 tsp freshly ground pepper, divided
1 tbsp extra-virgin olive oil

1/4 C. chopped dried apricots
1 tbsp minced fresh ginger
1 1/4 C. water
1 C. whole-wheat couscous
1 lb. salmon fillet, preferably wild Pacific, skinned and cut into 4 portions
2 tbsp chopped toasted cashews

## Directions

1. Set your grill for medium-high heat and lightly, grease the grill grate.
2. In a bowl, mix together the yogurt, scallion greens, lemon juice, cilantro, cumin, 1/4 tsp of the salt and 1/4 tsp of the pepper and keep aside.
3. In a large pan, heat the oil on medium heat and cook the apricots, ginger, the scallion whites and 1/4 tsp of the salt for about 2 minutes, stirring continuously.
4. Add the water and bring to a boil on high heat.
5. Stir in the couscous and remove from the heat.
6. Keep aside, covered for about 5 minutes.
7. With a fork, fluff the couscous mixture.
8. Meanwhile, season the salmon with the remaining salt and pepper.
9. Cook on the grill for about 3 minutes per side.
10. Serve alongside the couscous with a topping of the yogurt sauce and cashews.

# THURSDAY'S
# Salmon Dinner

Prep Time: 30 mins
Total Time: 42 mins

Servings per Recipe: 2
| | |
|---|---|
| Calories | 377 kcal |
| Fat | 13.6 g |
| Carbohydrates | 21.6g |
| Protein | 44 g |
| Cholesterol | 75 mg |
| Sodium | 768 mg |

## Ingredients

1 tsp olive oil
1/3 C. chopped onion
1 clove garlic, minced
salt and ground black pepper to taste
1/4 wedge lemon
water to cover
1 tbsp miso paste
1/4 cube vegetable bouillon
2 (6 oz.) skin-on salmon fillets

10 baby bok choy
2 carrots, cut into matchsticks
2 ribs celery, cut into matchsticks
1 bunch enoki mushrooms, cut from stalk
and separated
1 small bunch watercress
2 green onions, sliced on the bias

## Directions

1. In a large, deep skillet, heat the olive oil on medium heat and sauté the onion and garlic for about 5 minutes. Stir in the salt and pepper.
2. Squeeze the lemon juice over the onion mixture and add the rind in the skillet.
3. Add enough water to fill the skillet halfway.
4. Stir in the miso paste and vegetable bouillon cube and top with the salmon fillets, skin-side down.
5. Add enough water to cover and bring to a boil.
6. Simmer for about 4 minutes.
7. Add the baby bok choy, carrots and celery and simmer for about 2-6 minutes.
8. With a slotted spoon, transfer the salmon fillets to shallow bowls.
9. Discard the lemon rind from the skillet.
10. Stir in the enoki mushrooms, watercress and green onions and cook till heated completely.
11. Divide the baby bok choy, carrots, celery, enoki mushrooms, watercress and green onions in the bowls with salmon fillets.
12. Pour hot broth on top and serve.

# *Shibuya* Salmon

Prep Time: 15 mins
Total Time: 35 mins

Servings per Recipe: 4

| | |
|---|---|
| Calories | 479 kcal |
| Fat | 18.9 g |
| Carbohydrates | 31.6g |
| Protein | 37.4 g |
| Cholesterol | 84 mg |
| Sodium | 1964 mg |

## Ingredients

1/2 C. miso
1/3 C. mirin (Japanese sweet rice wine)
1/4 C. sake (Japanese rice wine)
3 tbsp firmly packed brown sugar
2 tbsp soy sauce

1 1/2 lb. salmon fillets
2 heads baby bok choy, halved lengthwise

## Directions

1. Set the broiler of your oven and arrange oven rack about 6-inches from the heating element.
2. Line a baking sheet with a piece of the foil paper.
3. In a shallow dish, mix together the miso, mirin, sake, brown sugar and soy sauce.
4. Add the salmon fillets and coat with the mixture evenly.
5. Keep aside for about 10-15 minutes in room temperature.
6. Remove the salmon fillets from the baking dish, reserving the marinade.
7. Place the salmon fillets onto the prepared baking sheet in a single layer.
8. Add the bok choy in the marinade and coat evenly.
9. Remove the salmon fillets from the baking dish, reserving the marinade.
10. Place the bok choy around the salmon fillets.
11. Cook under the broiler for about 4 minutes.
12. Flip the salmon fillets and bok choy and coat with the reserved marinade and cook for about 3 minutes.
13. Transfer the salmon fillets into the serving plates.
14. Cook the bok choy for about 3-4 minutes more.

# ENJOY THE RECIPES?

## KEEP ON COOKING
### WITH 6 MORE FREE COOKBOOKS!

Visit our website and simply enter your email address to join the club and receive your 6 cookbooks.

http://booksumo.com/magnet

 https://www.instagram.com/booksumopress/

https://www.facebook.com/booksumo/

Made in the USA
Las Vegas, NV
07 December 2023

82261539R00066